YOUR WILL'S COMPANION

By James H. Beauchamp

**A Product of
BGCJ Productions, LLC**

ISBN 978-0-578-14481-8

TABLE OF CONTENTS

Dedication:

To my clients, who have shared their lives with me –
their triumphs, their sorrows, their children, their
investments, their faith, their grief. My life is richer
because you told me your stories. Your wisdom has
hopefully helped me to be a better lawyer.

Your Will's Companion

Prologue

What do you mean, my will doesn't control how my IRA will be distributed? That can't be right. *But it is right.*

And you're telling me I have no control over how my IRA is to be paid to my kids? *If they are named as beneficiaries under your IRA, your kids control how much they receive, not you. The government has trumped your choices.*

No one ever told me that before.

Surprise, surprise.

Life is full of surprises, and most of them aren't what we wanted or planned for. There is no guaranty that this book will eliminate the element of surprise, in the realm of wills and estate planning, but we will give you some tips, some information, and some links to data, which should be of help to you and your family.

Since this is written with the thought that you might have bought a DIY will program or app (and in some respects, this book can be regarded as a User Manual for WillCrafter Lite, a DIY will available on most smart phones and tablets). This book should give you comfort in what you've done (or perhaps, force you to re-do your DIY will), based on the added information you will learn from this book.

Having a will is essential, regardless of whatever estate planning you have done in the past. But you need to consider a host of other things, such as your own retirement, planning around disabilities, considering prenuptial agreements if you remarry, avoiding probate, and so forth. So this "Companion" to your will is a treatise on a variety of topics.

Here's the organizational pattern: first, an eagle eye view of estate planning; next, a blow by blow explanation of wills, trusts, and the like, WHICH YOU SHOULD READ; third, a potpourri of information about federal estate taxes, selecting trustees (if you have a trust), naming beneficiaries of IRAs, who should serve as successor trustee of a trust, long term care, and a little information on retirement planning.

This book is about you and your family and your heirs, death taxes, income taxes, expenses, and retirement. You may jump to the sections that are of interest to you. If you are doing your will, with a computer program or app, please read Chapters 1, 2 and 3.

Chapter 1: TIPS IN ESTATE PLANNING

Smart estate planning involves more than having a will, even a fairly complex one. We are faced with continuing uncertainty in dealing with federal estate taxes, restrictive privacy rules in health care matters, mandated rules on how IRA and retirement accounts must be paid to beneficiaries, concerns over nursing home costs, and other financial privacy issues. With all of these factors in play, estate planning is a bit more complex than in years past.

You must take into account a realistic assessment of your net worth, retirement plans, and consider the possible impact of future estate taxes (although with $5,000,000 exemptions from federal estate taxes, which apply for persons dying during 2013 and thereafter, and with no estate taxes in the majority of cases, estate taxes are not a factor for most people).

This portion of the book deals with several topics, the first of which deals with estate and income taxes. Trusts, wills, and other topics are discussed later on.

The Estate Tax Component. The starting point begins with an assessment of your actual net worth. This assessment will also give you a fair indication of how much your estate might have to pay in death (or estate) taxes (this will not be a problem for most of us; estate taxes may be a problem if an estate value exceeds $5,000,000). If you are married, through the use of the portability rules, both you and your spouse can combine exemptions, so as to pass $10MM in assets to heirs, without any federal estate taxes.

As things now stand, there are no federal estate taxes for persons dying in 2010, and thereafter; estates with less than $5,000,000 are not taxed. If an estate exceeds $5,000,000, the estate tax rate is a flat 40%. FYI, the $5,000,000 is inflation indexed, and for the year 2013, the exemption is $5,250,000 (using the "portability rules", a married couple can pass wealth totaling $10,500,000 without any federal estate taxes – and without a credit sheltered trust).

Income Taxes. In addition, income taxes must be paid by your heirs, if they are the beneficiaries of your retirement plans (such as IRAs, 401k's, 403B's, etc.; but this tax does not apply to Roth IRAs). You cannot control how retirement benefits are paid to your heirs because the federal government has preempted your choices (there is one exception, which deals with naming a trust, or non-human being, as the beneficiary, and if that is the case, and in most cases, the trust will pay income taxes on benefits it receives at the 39.5% income tax bracket). Once you name a human being as your IRA beneficiary, the beneficiary will receive an annual payment from the plan administrator, which is be based on the life expectancy of the beneficiary (side note: if a beneficiary elects not to take a payout based on his or her life expectancy, they may do so, but will probably wind up paying more income taxes, based on a shorter withdrawal period, not to exceed 5 years).

So What Are We to Conclude on Estate Taxes?
Estate tax problems generally will not arise until your spouse dies. Anything you and your spouse collectively own which is worth over $5,000,000 will be subject to 40% estate taxes. If you have no surviving spouse (i.e., you are single, or your spouse died before 2011), your estate will not be taxed if your assets are less than $5,000,000.

Trusts. Most people like to control their own affairs, which is to say, they do not like the concept of probate. Probate is a court procedure, in effect in all 50 states, which deals with administration of your property after you die. Sometimes the costs of probate are very expensive, and sometimes, there are long delays before your estate is distributed to your heirs.

As a means of avoiding probate, many people place property in a trust. A trust is simply a written agreement as to how property will be held while you are alive, and what happens to the property when you die. You will be in charge of all property placed in a trust until you die (or are mentally incapacitated), and normally, you can change the provisions of a trust with less formality than amending a will. Here is a list of some of the benefits of owning property in trust:

- Because you can change a trust whenever you wish during your lifetime, it can adapt to changes in your needs and those of your family. The provisions of a trust do not become irrevocable until your death.

- In addition, such trusts can also save on fees and administrative expenses after your death, and save time and trouble for the beneficiaries. Assets can be paid out quickly after death, because trusts sidestep the sometimes costly and time-consuming probate process.

- Furthermore, in most instances, a displeased relative cannot contest the trust's provisions (as they can if you use a will – a will contest could hold up distribution of your estate for months or even years in probate court). To contest a trust, a disgruntled relative would have to file civil suits against each of the beneficiaries and/or the trustee. In many trusts, a contesting beneficiary will lose his or her potential inheritance, because the trust contains a no contest clause (which directs the trustee to pay the disgruntled beneficiary the sum of $10, or some other nominal amount).

- To set up the trusts you pay a one-time fee. Unless you later decide to change them, there are no further costs.

- Trusts also are strictly private affairs, unlike probate proceedings, which are matters of public record.

- If you later become incapacitated and are unable to handle your affairs, a correctly drawn trust can take care of your needs and those of your family without having to go through the court system to establish a guardianship. This means that many of your financial affairs can be handled far more expeditiously. For example, if a stock you own is failing, it can be sold quickly, rather than waiting for days or weeks until a court gives its approval. This, of course, can mean the difference between profits and losses.

The Trustees. You'll undoubtedly name yourself as trustee of your trust, but you'll also have to choose one or more successor trustees to handle your affairs if you can't, and distribute the trust estate after you die.

You may want to name your spouse as co-trustee or successor trustee, if he or she has a good head for business, but you'll still need someone else to take over if you and your spouse both die in a common accident. The first consideration, obviously, is that the person must be trustworthy, whether the person is a family member, close friend, or professional, such as your accountant, perhaps your lawyer, or a member of your bank's trust department.

If you'd like to name a relative but fear there may be too much pressure and quarreling within your family, it's probably a good idea to name an institution or a professional to handle the job.

As a safeguard, the trust should contain a provision that allows you to remove any successor trustee, for whatever reason, and name another at your discretion. After your death, the trust is irrevocable, and the question then becomes, can your trust beneficiaries remove the person or institution you have named as successor trustees? No, in most instances. Some trusts have provisions dealing with removal of successor trustees, but you get to make those rules.

Funding the Trust. To avoid probate – which is a highly desirable objective – the Settlors (sometimes referred to as Grantors or Trustors or Trust Makers – in other words, the persons establishing the trust) of a revocable living trust must transfer all right, title and interest to their property, to a Trustee. The probate court will not have jurisdiction over the trust, if your trust is properly "funded" with assets. Stated differently, the probate court only has jurisdiction over your property if it is titled in one of three ways: (a) in an individual name; (b) as a tenant in common with another; or (c) whenever a life insurance policy, an interest in a pension or retirement plan, or an IRA, designates the death beneficiary as being "my estate". All other types of property – life insurance which designates a beneficiary other than "my estate", property owned as joint tenants with right of survivorship (or tenancy by the entireties), or property held in trust or property which has a pay on death beneficiary or a transfer on death beneficiary – escape the jurisdiction of the Probate Court.

Thus, to avoid probate, title to (most of) your property must be transferred to a Trustee.

In a properly drawn revocable living trust, there are certain assets which are listed, which are deemed to be property belonging to the trust estate – without any other specific document of conveyance to a Trustee. For instance, personal property owned by the Settlor at the time of his or her decease, unless specifically excluded, should be regarded as being a trust asset. Clothes owned by the Settlor would fall within the category of tangible personal property, and such property would belong to the trust estate (when you sign the trust, you will probably sign a bill of sale or assignment of the personal property, to the trust). Similarly, household goods would fall within the list.

Real Estate. The problem of funding the trust becomes a bit more complicated with respect to real estate. In all instances where a trust is prepared, and the Settlor owns real property, a quit claim deed (i.e., a grant deed, made without warranty as to title issues) is usually signed, in which title is conveyed from the Settlor to the Trustee. If the Trustee dies, then the Successor Trustee will sign an affidavit (also known as a Certificate of Incumbency, or Memorandum of Trust) and file it with the Registrar of Deeds. Such an affidavit should be sufficient evidence to satisfy a title examiner that the trust was not revoked prior to the Settlor's death and that the duties of Trustee are now being carried on by a Successor Trustee. By analogy, if the president of a corporation resigns, the corporate by-laws provide the vice president assumes the office of president. Similarly, a Successor Trustee assumes the duties of the office of Trustee, when the original Trustee no longer serves in that capacity (due to death or incapacity).

In most instances, the Settlors will record the quit claim deed with the Registrar of Deeds (i.e., the County Clerk). Once the deed is recorded, the County Tax Assessor might argue that the homestead exemption of the Settlor is lost because title in the real estate is being held by a Trustee, not a homesteader. This issue varies from state to state, and you should consider calling your local county assessor, to determine what the local rules are on the homestead exemption, and whether you can expect to pay extra real estate taxes, if the property is placed in trust.

In a few instances, the land will be subject to restrictions against transfer. The prime example is land owned by Native Americans (in real estate law, the general topic is known as "Indian Land Law"). The Bureau of Indian Affairs must approve the transfer, and in some instances, the Indian Nation must also approve the transfer (such as the Osage Tribe).

In addition to real estate, Settlors should also convey title to the

Trustees, to any interest in mortgages (and the notes which are secured by the mortgage), time shares, and oil and gas interests.

Stocks and Bonds. But what about title to other types of properties, such as stocks and bonds? Here's what happens when a trust is "unfunded". Several years ago, a client owned several millions of dollars in securities. The client (who was the Settlor of the trust) died without first transferring title to the securities to the Trustee (he was the trustee). He died, and the successor trustee then called and asked what she must do to get the securities in her dad's trust. This was in 1984, and things were a bit different then. I explained to her that her dad should have put his brokerage account in his name as trustee of the trust. I then learned that he did not have a stock broker, but only had stock certificates.

When I told her his will had to be admitted to probate, she hit the roof: she didn't want her friends to search the probate records, which are open to the public, and learn that she was a millionaire. She asked if I could convince the stock transfer agents for all of these companies that when her dad signed his trust, he conveyed his stock interest to himself as trustee of the trust. There was some language in the trust which suggested that a conveyance had been made, so I gave it a try.

I began a time consuming telephone and letter campaign with lots of stock transfer agents. After banging some heads, and citing the rules of the stock transfer association (which were only 20 pages long at the time; now the rules are at least 100 pages long), I was able to cajole the stock transfer agents that the stock was transferred to the trust. In retrospect, we were lucky.

To avoid this sort of problem, the Settlor should at least sign a stock power or an allonge (which is an endorsement to the stock certificate, and works much the same way as a stock power) as part of the trust closing documents – and the signature of the Settlor (as shown on the stock power or allonge) should be guaranteed by an officer of a national banking institution, using the Medallion Guaranty stamp (this is a nationally recognized signature guaranty program). An easier method would be to have the stock certificates kept by a stock broker. The brokerage account would be in the name of the trust (i.e., the trustees; technically speaking, only trustees can own property – the trustees hold the property in trust, for the benefit of the beneficiaries).

In addition, it would be helpful if the Settlors maintained a list of all of the trust assets, including all stock certificates, bonds, life insurance policies, by date of issue and registration or policy number, etc., as well as a list of title certificates for automobiles, horses, airplanes, mobile homes, boats, bank accounts, or anything else that has a registration number. Such a list would be additional proof of what assets were included in the trust, and such a list would be of tremendous benefit to the successor trustee (who really ought to know what you own when you die).

Other options on stock. As an alternative means of avoiding probate, the owner might make a "transfer on death" designation (this requires contacting the stock transfer agent or stock broker and completing additional forms), and indicate that upon the death of the owner, the security or brokerage account will be "transferred on death" (TOD) to the acting trustee of the trust.

Bank Accounts. All bank accounts and bank account numbers, regardless of the style of the account, should be included in the trust, as being part of the trust assets. It is advisable to change the style of the account at the bank, and this can be accomplished as follows: (a) the Settlors can re-title their account as being a trust account (this method is usually the only means available at a credit union – and some banks will not permit the account to be styled any other way) – new checks will not have to be printed, because the account will not be regarded as a "new" account; or (b) the Settlors can add a POD (pay on death) designation to the account, with "the acting trustee of the Smith Revocable Living Trust" as being the POD beneficiary (this method is permitted by most banks) – again, no new checks will be required. The taxpayer identification number for the account will be one of the Settlors' social security numbers.

When you die, the bank account will be owned by your trust, and the successor trustee you name in your trust will have to prove you died before taking over the account (the trustee will have to show the bank your death certificate, and sign a document which states that he, she or it has assumed the duties of trustee of your trust).

IRA's and Retirement Plans. Because there are income taxes to be paid on retirement plans (except Roth IRA's), even in the event of death, there may be adverse income tax consequences to the beneficiaries if a death beneficiary has been improperly designated. Normally, the plan participant will name his or her surviving spouse as the primary death beneficiary, with the children named as contingent beneficiaries. These benefits will be paid independently of what the trust states, because the trust never owns the IRAs. The benefits are usually paid to the named beneficiary, over that beneficiary's life expectancy. The beneficiary may elect to receive distribution over a 5 year period (or less), instead of over his or her life expectancy (you cannot control this, however; the designated beneficiary controls payout).

Insurance. The beneficiary of insurance policies will normally be the acting trustee of the trust (in some instances, the other spouse will be the primary beneficiary, with the acting trustee as a contingent beneficiary). There are no adverse income tax consequences to receiving life insurance (the policy proceeds are not taxed for income tax purposes; the only exception to this is the Transfer for Value rule, which basically means you were not the original beneficiary, but bought the beneficial interest from the original beneficiary). If the life insurance proceeds are paid to the trust, the trustee can hold the proceeds for a named beneficiary, until the beneficiary attains a desired age (e.g., Little Billie will get his share of the trust, but not until he is 25 years old; until then, the trustee can make payments to him or for his benefit).

Annuities. There may or may not be income tax ramifications on the death benefits of an annuity, depending on whether the annuity has grown in value since you bought it. However, the death beneficiary of an annuity should normally be a human being, rather than a trust. There are usually adverse income tax benefits if the annuity is payable to a trust (even if the trust owns the annuity).

Power of Attorney. Another estate planning instrument you'll need is a durable power of attorney that usually designates the agent as being the same person you've selected as your successor trustee. A power of attorney, which creates an agency relationship between the principal and his or her attorney in fact, isn't a magic document that will take the place of wills and trusts, because it's automatically revoked at death. However, a "durable power of attorney," if permissible where you live, will allow the person you've chosen to act for you (i.e., as your agent), if you're unable to do so yourself (which usually means, during periods of mental disability). This is especially helpful if you or your spouse must go into a nursing home or some other institution (and in this instance, a health care power of attorney is usually signed; the health care agent might be someone different from the financial agent you have named under the durable power of attorney).

Living Will. You may also want to have a "living will" that says you don't want to be kept on a life support system if you're terminally ill or there's no hope of recovery. Most states allow this choice. These documents may also permit donation of body parts to science. Keep in mind that "one size does not fit all"; every state uses a different form.

Business Owners. If you own a business, you have still more planning to do, because control of the business must be carefully planned, and your family taken care of. You'll probably have to answer some hard questions in designing a business succession program. For example, do you have:

- A procedure, acceptable to IRS, to value the stock in your closely held business?
- A buy-sell agreement with a potential purchaser of the company stock?
- Life insurance that is earmarked specifically to fund the buy-sell agreement?
- A "key man" insurance policy that will help your company procure new management?
- An asset that will provide cash to pay estate taxes that will be due on your death?

Other means of dealing with an estate. A revocable trust can't protect you from creditors, or give you any benefit if you need help on paying for nursing home costs. There are, however, other means of passing title to property without a will or trust (using a transfer on death deed, or POD bank account). These techniques in property ownership don't help if you are disabled, and for that, you need a durable power of attorney.

SUMMARY

Estate planning requires some thinking on your part, and you should learn as much as you can about how your property can be distributed when you die. If you die without a will or trust, your estate will be distributed to your heirs, based on a formula the legislature has established. To resolve this uncertainty, your should at least have a will. Keep in mind that the probate of an estate is not an evil undertaking, which should be avoided at all costs. However, it is time-consuming and in many instances, very expensive for the heirs. Hopefully some of the concepts mentioned in this part of the book will be of assistance in the estate planning process.

Chapter 2: DOING IT YOURSELF

Many will decide to do their own wills, or make their own variations of computer and internet generated wills. Hopefully, this will work. But one of the purposes of this book is to give you background material, so that you will know with reasonable certainty how your property will be distributed.

In most instances, no one wants to read an instruction manual on how to do your own estate planning, specifically, your will. The problem that you might be creating is this: your will might not be valid, which means, you will die, and distribution of your estate will be determined by how your state legislature thinks your estate should be distributed.

To help you do it yourself (DIY), we will give you background on a host of topics. For organizational purposes, think of making a will as a set of building blocks: the blocks must be put together in the right order.

WillCrafter (the iPad app) and WillCrafter Lite (smart phone and iPad app) are designed to force you to put your will together in the correct order. If you bought another app or computer program, you can still use the methodology used in WillCrafter; think of a will as a set of building blocks. The blocks should be in the right order, and each block should contain enough information, so as to make your will understandable to a judge.

Regardless of the DIY app you are using, don't sign it until you have two witnesses (who are over 18, are competent, not related to you, and are not named as the beneficiaries under your will or of your estate) see you sign it (they will "attest" they saw you sign). In addition, in some states you'll need a notary public.

Once you have assembled all of these people, tell them you are signing the document as your last will and testament, and that you want them to witness what you are doing. Sign the will wherever a signature is required on the form you are using (one state, Louisiana, requires you to sign your name at the bottom of each page).

Since each state has its own set of rules for signing a will, we have given you a spreadsheet to use, in locating the rules for all 50 states and the District of Columbia. Go to this internet site: www.willcrafter.com/state_law_summary.xlsx. Some states give you specific language to use, and others do not.

After the will has been signed, keep it in a safe place. When you die, your heirs will have to get it admitted to probate, so that your estate will be distributed how you specified in your will.

So what are the things I should know, in order to create my own, valid and enforceable will?

1. **Each state has its own set of rules** dealing with who is eligible to create a will, the formalities of making and signing a will, and what should be in a will. Let's go down the list.

First, you must be old enough to sign a will. Although this age requirement varies from state to state, we suggest you should not sign a will unless you are 18 years old.

When you get around to preparing your will, it should say that it is your last will and testament, and that you revoke all other wills you might have made beforehand (including amendments, which are known as codicils).

2. **The will should indicate where you live**, because a will is normally probated in that state. If you live in Michigan, but sign a will in Ohio, must you follow Ohio law on signing wills, or Michigan's? The answer is Ohio. The validity of the will is

determined by the state law where it is signed.

3. **It is a good idea to give your family tree in the will**: indicate whether you are single or married, whether you have children, including children born out of wedlock and children who predeceased you (if the predeceased child leaves children, then name them). In addition, include the names of any of your children who have been adopted by others (in most states, those children are entitled to inherit from biological parents and adoptive parents; if you disinherit a child, it is a good idea to give that child the sum of $1, so they cannot later complain they were overlooked). If you have entered into a civil union or same sex marriage, you should mention that, too.

4. **You need to appoint someone who will be in charge of your estate after you die**. That person or trust company is known as an executor, independent executor, or personal representative. Those terms mean the same thing. In addition, you should state that the executor is to serve without bond. If you do not mention the topic of bonds in your will, the court will require the executor to buy a fidelity bond, which is not easy to come by. To procure such a bond, insurance companies (who issue the bonds) may want the executor to post a certificate of deposit payable to the insurance company or buy an irrevocable letter of credit, to serve as security for the bond. The purpose of the bond is obvious: if the personal representative steals from the estate, the insurance company will cover the loss.

To avoid this unnecessary and expensive procedure, you should simply state that you request the personal representative serve without bond.

5. **If you have minor children, you should appoint a guardian for those children**. If you're married, your spouse will usually be the guardian of your children. If both you and your spouse die, then the guardian you name will serve in one of two capacities: first, the Guardian of the person is responsible for

the physical well being of the minor. The guardian of the estate, also known as guardian of the property, is in charge of whatever inheritance the minor child might receive. That guardian will be supervised by the court, and with the court's permission, will use the inherited property until the child reaches age 18, or in many states, will simply hold the money until the child reaches age 18. In all instances, the guardian will have to file an annual report as to the ward's condition (the ward is the person under the guardianship) and itemize how the money was spent, invested, etc.

You can establish a testamentary trust for the minor child (this means, the will sets up a trust for the minor child). The trustee of the testamentary trust will presumably be the same person as Guardian of the estate (or property). The trustee distributes the property as you have specified in the will (some states require annual trustee reports be filed with the Probate Court). If you want the property to be used for education only, the Guardian/trustee will be limited on spending the money for that purpose. The trust can continue past age 18, if you so desire.

6. **If the beneficiary of your will is disabled**, that person might lose government benefits, if you leave them too much money. In most instances you can create a special needs trust, so the inherited property will not disqualify the beneficiary from receiving government benefits. The topic of special needs trusts is beyond the scope of this book, but you should investigate this topic on your own (if one of your beneficiaries is disabled or is receiving government benefits).

7. **In the will you also need to state how you want your property to be distributed when you die.** If you make a specific gift, which is known as a bequest, you can list the property, and give instructions to the personal representative to distribute that property to a specified person.

At some point in the will, you will distribute the "rest, remainder and residue" of your estate to persons or organizations. Make certain that the fractional amounts or the percentages distributed equals 100.

8. **Except for your spouse or pretermitted heirs (that is, children you are not mentioning in the will), you can disinherit children**. In many states you can add a penalty clause on persons who might contest the will, by stating that such contestants will receive $1. Many states do not enforce such penalty clauses, and the will can simply state: I intentionally make no provision for any other person who is not named herein as a devisee or legatee, but if someone contests this will because his or her name is not mentioned, or I have not given such person any part of my estate, then I give such person the sum of $1.

9. **If one of the devisees or legatees or residual beneficiaries dies before you, that share will go to his or her issue** (children), parents, brothers, sisters, etc.; the rules determining who inherits the share is found in the statute of descent and distribution (your state legislature has determined this for you). To avoid that uncertainty, your will can state that if Person A dies before you, that share shall be distributed to Person B.

10. **Formalities in Signing a Will.** The will needs to be signed and witnessed (by two disinterested, competent persons), and special language must be used in the will (normally, the witnesses sign under the attestation clause). Each state has a different set of rules on attestation. In addition, and in most states, a will can be self proved, which means the witnesses are not required to show up in court and testify that they saw you sign the will (some states even combine the concepts of attestation and self proving). Generally speaking, if a will is self-proved, a notary will have to be present when you sign the will. The verbiage in your will dealing with attestation and "self proving" must be correct. Go to the internet site: http://www.willcrafter.com/state_law_summary.xlsx, and use it to locate the rules in your state. You may have to read more

than you want to, but you can compare your DIY signature rules with the statute (if you are using WillCrafter, some state statutes, such as Arkansas, may not give an explicit form to use; the language in WillCrafter and WillCrafter Lite have been adapted to meet the state rules).

In some states, you are permitted to have other people sign the will for you (providing you direct them to do so). We don't cover this topic in this book (we are trying to help you and your heirs from getting into lawsuits).

11. **Estate Taxes.** If your estate is large enough, there may be an estate tax (which generally applies to persons other than your spouse – providing your spouse is a US citizen); estate taxes and inheritance taxes also known as death taxes.

There are techniques available to double the amount of the federal estate tax exemption, which is $5,000,000 (for those dying in 2010 and thereafter; this amount is inflation indexed, which means, if you die in 2013, the exemption is $5,250,000). One method of doubling the exemption, for a married couple, is to create a credit shelter trust (you will need a lawyer to help you do that). Another method is to use the "portability rules", which requires the surviving spouse to file a federal estate tax return, when his or her spouse dies (I know this is expensive, but by doing this, the exemption for your children is $10,000,000, instead of $5,000,000; the estate tax savings could be $2,000,000, i.e., 40% of $5,000,000).

This book does not provide much information on sheltered trusts, or other esoteric concepts, such as special needs trusts, income cap trusts, and provisions dealing with generation skipping transfer taxes. If your estate is more than $5,000,000, please discuss estate planning with a lawyer, CPA, or a financial planner. Read on for a cursory discussion about credit sheltered trusts and the portability rules.

12. **Credit sheltered trusts and the Portability Rules.** The objective of a credit sheltered trust is to double the federal estate tax exemption, but this can only work if you are married. The mechanics of doing this are somewhat complicated, but in your will, you should leave the bulk of your estate to your spouse. When you die, part of what you own will be put in a sub-trust, known as a credit sheltered trust, and this will equal the federal estate tax exemption (it is $5,120,000 in 2012, and $5,250,000 in 2013). Your spouse or children, or a combination, will receive this part of your estate. The rest of your estate is placed in another sub-trust, which qualifies for the marital deduction (this is a deduction permitted under federal estate tax law), and this amount will not be taxed on your death, since you're leaving it to your spouse. When your spouse dies, the spouse will include whatever is left in the marital share, in his or her taxable estate – but the spouse will also receive a credit towards estate taxes (it is $5,120,000 in 2012, and $5,250,000 in 2013). The amount placed in the credit sheltered trust (also called the by-trust, or the family trust) is not taxed, for estate taxes.

Thus, you can double the amount of the tax exemption, at the federal level, by use of the credit sheltered trust.

Portability Rules. If you do not have a credit sheltered trust, you can still enjoy the "doubling of exemption" benefit, through the Portability Rules. When the first spouse dies, a federal estate tax return is filed, whether or not there is a tax to pay. If husbands and wives give all of their estates to each other, on the first death, then the Portability Rules, permit doubling the exemption, on the second death.

This somewhat abbreviated version of the rule should be discussed with your CPA or estate planning lawyer, because estates of over $5,000,000 should not be using DIY wills.

13. **Generation Skipping Transfer Tax.** If you leave a vast amount of property to grandchildren, your estate may have to pay

a generation skipping transfer tax. This tax is a penal tax, which is about 22% higher than the top marginal estate tax bracket (this might be from 62% – 70% of the amount going to the grandchildren). The good news is that it doesn't come into play, unless the gifts to grandchildren are more than $5,120,000 (for the year 2012; if you die in 2012 and thereafter, gifts are taxed if they are over $5,250,000). There are other rules and considerations (such as the annual exclusion of $14,000), but generation skipping transfer taxes are too complicated to discuss in this short book.

14. **IRAs and Retirement Plans.** Wills don't control IRAs, 401ks, and the like; whoever you designate as a beneficiary of the IRA receives what's there, because you have named them as beneficiaries on your IRA beneficiary designation form. Your will doesn't control that part of your estate.

The IRA beneficiary will pay income taxes on what they receive (unless you have a ROTH IRA). Spouses can defer the income taxes in certain cases, but your kids cannot (they can stretch out the benefits, to lessen the income tax burden in a given year, but they cannot roll your IRA over to their IRA, in the same manner your spouse can). Since IRAs and the like are controlled by your IRA beneficiary designation form, we won't mention this topic again.

15. **Property not controlled by wills**. Wills may name the people you want to receive your estate, but they don't control beneficiary designations on annuities, life insurance, IRAs and retirement plans, brokerage accounts where you have designated a transfer on death beneficiary (TOD beneficiary), bank accounts where you have designated a pay on death beneficiary (POD beneficiary), nor do wills control property you own as a joint tenant with another person (or persons), or as tenants by the entireties, or accounts known as "Totten trusts".

As an example, if your will states "I give, devise and bequeath the rest, remainder and residue of my estate to my beloved wife, Susie", but you have designated Hanna Hagworth as the beneficiary of your IRA, Hanna gets the IRA. Susie won't be pleased if she survives you and learns the bulk of your estate has been left to someone else, but the will cannot trump the IRA designation.

16. **Burial requests**. Unless your state law gives credence to burial requests in an expedited fashion, keep in mind that It may take a month or longer to get a will admitted to probate (meaning, the Court has accepted your will as being valid). For this reason, it is probably not a good idea to give burial instructions in your will.

17. **Complex wills**. You will have lots of choices to make if you use any DIY will app or program. However, most DIY will programs or apps will not cover what we consider as extremely complicated scenarios.

18. **Statutory wills**. A few states (such as California) have statutory forms, which you should feel to use instead of a DIY computer generated will. However, the concepts in this book should be of use, even if you use your state's statutory form.

19. **Legal advice.** This book has been written by a lawyer, but there is no attorney-client relationship created, even though you have read the book from cover to cover. We are not giving you legal advice, nor are we offering to make a will for you. Since we are not a law firm, there is no attorney client relationship established. The document you prepare as a DIY will must be conformed to your state law, as far as signatures needed, attestation, and in some instances, paragraphs which "self prove" the will.

Some of you will show your handiwork to a lawyer (who may even be your friend). We cannot guarantee your lawyer will approve of your DIY will, but the information contained in this book is designed so that you can prepare your own will, which can be admitted to probate when you die.

Chapter 3: MORE SPECIFICS ON WILLS AND TRUSTS (and examples for your consideration)

A little knowledge is a dangerous thing, so says Alexander Pope or Francis Bacon. Now that you have read the summary portion of the book, the question you should be asking yourself, do I know enough to complete a DIY will? Let us help you critique the situation: read the sections below, to give yourself comfort (or discomfort). Each section should broaden your horizons, in matters of estate planning, and ought to help you make much needed plans for you and your loved ones.

Wills. A will is a document you sign, normally in the presence of witnesses, and sometimes before a notary public. Your will simply gives instructions on how your estate will be distributed when you die.

There is an old saying that a "will speaks at the time of death". Conceptually, this means you can change your will at almost any time, right up to the time you die. You have to be competent, be of legal age, and act of your own free volition (no guns pointed at your head, with someone telling you where to sign). In legalese, when you sign a will, you cannot be defrauded, under duress or undue influence (forged wills don't work either).

Except for handwritten wills (and in some cases, handwritten wills must be witnessed), all wills must be witnessed, which is a safeguard against forgery. Depending on how the will is prepared (handwritten or typed), you may or may not need witnesses. The will needs to be dated and signed by you.

If you are married, and if it is permitted by your state law, you can sign a joint will (this is known as a conjoint and mutual will). We don't recommend this method of doing things, because when one person dies, the surviving spouse is bound by a will he or she can't change (the will is irrevocable). Conjoint and mutual wills are not covered in this book.

The first information needed in creating a will is identifying who you are: your full legal name, and the state where you live. Here's an example:

Last Will and Testament

My name is _____. I reside in _____, and I am of sound mind and memory, and I desire to make proper provision for the distribution of my entire estate when I die. I hereby declare and publish this to be my Last Will and Testament, and I hereby revoke any and all Wills and codicils (amendments) I have previously made.

Why all of this language? First, you want everyone to know this is your last will and testament (you might have signed a will at an earlier date, but this one is your final and current version). Second, you want everyone to know that you are revoking wills and amendments you might have made at an earlier date. Third, you want everyone to know you are mentally alert, etc., and that you reside in one of the 50 states or the District of Columbia.

Caution: The verbiage and phraseology used in a will are there for a reason. Don't alter the text suggested in this book very much.

At this point, you may be thinking, why not forget the whole thing? Well, if you die without a will, your state legislature has written a will for you: this law is normally outlined in the Statute of Descent and Distribution. Each state has a different law, but generally, many legislatures believe that half (or at least a portion) of your estate should go to your spouse, and the remainder to your children. If you are single without children, then your estate will be divided between your siblings, perhaps your parents, nieces, nephews, cousins, and so forth. To prevent this from happening – you have to prepare and sign a will, which will dictate how your estate is to be distributed.

Why have a will? I thought we answered this question on the previous pages. But here it is again, and here is your answer: you have a will so you can control how your property is to be split up (distributed), when you die.

So how does this work? After you die, does everyone crowd in a room, and sit attentively while a lawyer "reads the will"? That can be done, of course, but it's a lot easier if the heirs are given a photocopy of the will, which they can read at their leisure.

After you die, the will has to go through the probate process. First, whenever you hear or read the word "probate", substitute the word "proved". In other words, the will has to be proved to be authentic, and thus, the will must grind its way through the "probate process", before your property is distributed.

The Probate Process. Each state has a probate court, though many states don't call their courts "probate courts". The probate procedure is even described by different names: consider Louisiana, where the process is generally referred to as Succession.

Once the will is admitted to probate (that is, proven to be authentic), the lawyer representing the estate will file quite a few papers before the estate can be closed and the property distributed to the heirs (the probate process can take as little time as a month in states like Texas – or probate process can last several decades, as satirized by Charles Dickens in *Bleak House*). Most probate cases can be concluded in less than a year.

That may not sound attractive to you, and later we will explain some techniques used to avoid probate. But bear with us. First there are some important things that ought to be dealt with in a will. Let's start with your family tree. Here's an example:

Family Status. I declare that I am married (single). My spouse is _____. I have ___ children, who are: _____, _____, _____, and _____. All are living (or, _____ predeceased me, and left surviving him/her the following children: _____, _____, and _____; or, _____ predeceased me, and left no children surviving him/her)

OR

I declare that I am single, and that my parents ___ and ___ are living (or, that my parents predeceased me, and I have ___ siblings, who are: ____ and ___ (if a sibling has died, then add, ____ is now deceased, and he/she is survived by ___ and ____, who are his/her children).

OR

I declare that I am not married but am in a civil union (or same sex marriage), and that my parents ___ and ___ are living (or, that my parents predeceased me, and I have ___ siblings, who are: ____ and ___ (if a sibling has died, then add, ____ is now deceased, and he/she is survived by ___ and ____, who are his/her children). My civil union (or same sex marriage) is with _____.

Definitions. As used in this Will, the terms "child", "children", "issue", "lawful issue", "descendant", or "descendants", shall include persons legally adopted. Where applicable, references in this Will to the masculine shall include the feminine and to the singular shall include the plural.

Other matters. I have intentionally made no provision for any child born after the date of this will, and furthermore, have intentionally made no provision for any spouse not mentioned herein, or any spouse I may have at the time of my death, or any other person not mentioned. If any portion of this will is invalid, for any reason, the remainder of the will shall nonetheless be considered as a valid last will and testament. Should any part of my will be determined to be unenforceable, the other parts of the will are valid and enforceable.

What if you leave someone out of your family tree?

And how deep must the family tree go?

If you are married, list your spouse. The adjunct to this concept is, you can't disinherit your spouse (the law is emerging in states where civil unions and same sex marriages are permitted, and we will not speculate whether a civil union "partner" or same sex spouse can be disinherited).

Let's return to traditional marriages: unless your spouse has signed a valid prenuptial agreement, and relinquishes his or her rights to inherit, the spouse can contest the will, should you give your spouse less than what he or she is entitled to receive under the statute of descent and distribution. If you leave your spouse less than the share permitted under the statute of descent and distribution, your spouse may contest your will, and elect to receive his or her statutory share (as determined by the laws of descent and distribution).

If you have children, list them, whether or not they were born out of wedlock. If one of your children has predeceased you, list the deceased child's children. If you have a child who has been adopted by someone else, mention that child in the family tree section of your will.

Can you disinherit a child? Yes, but read on. Some states have pretermitted heir laws. Pretermitted means to omit or disregard. If you live in a state like Oklahoma, and don't mention one of your children (or adopted children) in your will, the omitted child (or his or her heirs, if your child died before you) can contest your will, and the judge is required to give that child his or her statutory share of your estate, regardless of what you have stated to the contrary in your will.

To be on the safe side, name all of your children, even those born out of wedlock (doing this will avoid a will contest, later on, brought by a child not mentioned in the will). Second, consider adding an in terrorem clause ("if anyone contests this will, that person shall receive $1) – these clauses aren't enforceable in every state, so to get around those states, simply give at least $1 to each of your children. Third, state "I intentionally make no provision for any children who may be born or adopted hereafter," or "If anyone, whether an heir of my estate or otherwise, contests this will and claims a right to inherit from me, then everyone should assume I have intentionally elected not to leave my estate to that person."

If you are single, list your parents, and indicate whether they are living or not. If they are deceased, then mention your siblings. If one of your siblings has died before you, mention whether they had children, and list your nieces and nephews.

You don't have to join a genealogy society to write a will. Most states only require you to go through two generations, if there are deceased relatives who should be included in your family tree.

And now last, but not least: civil unions and same sex marriages. If you have entered into a civil union or same sex marriage, should this information go on the "truncated" family tree, which is part of your will? It won't hurt to list the civil union partner or same sex spouse, but the statutes of descent and distribution in your state may not even mention the topic of civil unions.

Here's what you might do: Mention the civil union or same sex marriage in the family tree portion of the will. When you later deal with how your estate is to be distributed, list the person's name, and state what percentage (including 100%) that person is to receive.

Remember, the concept of civil unions and same sex marriages is relatively new, and the states permitting civil unions and same sex marriages don't always include the concept in the statute of descent and distribution (persons named in the statute of descent and distribution inherit your estate when you die without a will; if your will isn't admitted to probate, they also inherit your estate, per the language in the statute).

Executors. You need to name the executor of your estate (we now call the executor by another phrase, which doesn't require you to know Latin: the personal representative). Here are some considerations:

If you don't use the right language in the will, your personal representative (the "PR") might not qualify to serve if his or her net worth is not as large as your estate. To save time and avoid the expense of having your PR purchase a fidelity bond (which will shore up his or her creditworthiness), you can ask the court to waive the requirement that the PR be bonded.

Personal Representatives are limited in what they can do. Each state gives the PR some statutory powers to do things, such as sign income tax returns for your final Form 1040, but normally, your PR will liquidate your estate and turn your property into cash (occasionally, the Probate Court judge will have to give the PR permission to sell your property). From these cash resources, your PR can then pay any bills that need to be paid (funeral expenses, costs of probate administration, credit cards, mortgages, car payments, etc.). The WillCrafter DIY will has added language which gives the PR powers, in addition to those your state might not have thought of (your legislature will give the PR certain "powers", such as filing an inventory, and these are known as "statutory powers").

Executors (Personal Representatives) are entitled to a fee for their services, which is either set by statute or by Court order. If you like, you may add a sentence limiting the fee to a percentage of your estate, or a fixed dollar amount.

If you appoint a thief as your Personal Representative (or a felon, or someone who is financially unstable, or someone who is mentally incompetent), the Court may deny your choice and select someone else. So pick someone who is trustworthy and untainted.

You ask, "What does a Personal Representative do?" Here's a partial list:

1. Select a lawyer to represent him or her (though there are exceptions to the rule, the legal system requires a lawyer to represent your estate).

2. The PR will follow the directions given by the lawyer.

3. The PR will take possession of what your owned when you died; he or she or it will list and give values for what you owned (this list generally doesn't include life insurance, annuities, retirement benefits, joint tenancy property which passes to the other joint tenants, or bank accounts or real estate or stock brokerage accounts which have a TOD (transfer on death) or POD (pay on death) beneficiary, or Totten trusts, which are treated the same as a POD account).

4. The PR will report to the Court, in writing, on what you owned when you died and how much the property was worth when you died (this report is normally called an Inventory; it doesn't include all the assets which don't go through probate; see paragraph 3).

5. The PR will send notices (letters) to your creditors, advising them to make claims (in writing) against your estate by a specified date. If the claims are approved by the PR, the PR will pay the bill (unless the estate is insolvent, in which case, the Court will approve who gets paid).

6. The PR will file tax returns for you and your estate (if your estate is large, there may be estate, inheritance and death taxes to be paid out of your resources).

7. After the passage of time, the PR will file a financial statement of what's been collected, what's been spent, what's left, and an indication of how the estate is to be distributed (this is generally known as a Final Account; interested parties can object to what's been done or what's proposed). If the judge approves this report, then the estate is distributed, and the probate is closed.

8. Probate court records are public documents, so anyone is entitled to see what has been done in a probate case.

9. Most of these rules don't apply in Texas, which has an expedited process. Once the will has been admitted to probate and the PR has been appointed (in Texas, the PR is known as the Independent Executor), the Court will order the Independent Executor to distribute the estate. Texas assumes the Independent Executor will pay the bills, sell the property, and distribute the estate without any court supervision.

FYI, you may name Co-Executors, if you prefer to do so. Here's an example:

> ***Appointment of Personal Representative and Successor.*** I nominate, constitute and appoint my spouse, _____, as Personal Representative of my estate under this, my Last Will and Testament, to serve without bond. In the event that he/she should predecease me or shall be unable to serve, I then designate _____ as substitute or successor Personal Representatives. I request that the Probate Court require no bond of my Substitute or Successor Personal Representatives. My Personal Representative(s) shall (collectively) receive a fee of no more than 2.25% of my probate estate, plus reimbursement for out of pocket expenses and advances.
> ***Powers of Personal Representative.*** My said Personal Representative shall have the power, in addition to and not

in modification of all common law and statutory power, and without obtaining any Order or other approval of any Court to settle and adjust all claims and demands in favor of or against my estate; to defer payment of any claim or portion thereof that is not due and payable; to retain any property in the same form or instrument as that in which it is received; to invest or reinvest principal and income in such securities or other property, real or personal as my said Personal Representative may deem advisable, without being limited to investments which fiduciaries are authorized by law to make; to determine whether money or property shall be considered income or principal or partly income and partly principal; to charge or apportion expenses and losses to principal or income as my said Personal Representative deems just and equitable; to manage, control, maintain, improve, lease for any term, rent, exchange, sell, convey and transfer at public or private sale, all or any part of the real or personal property comprising my estate, for such prices and upon such terms as my said Personal Representative deems advisable, and to execute and deliver proper instruments of conveyance and transfer; to execute and deliver proxies, powers of attorney and such other instruments as are incident to the holding, control and voting of corporate securities or the sale or exchange thereof; to borrow money and to execute promissory notes and use any property of my estate as security therefor; to make any division or distribution in money, in kind, or partly in each, and in making any such division or interest therein, to any person, although different in kind from property allocated or distributed to any other person; to create such reserves out of income as such Personal Representative deems advisable for depreciation, obsolescence, amortization and to insure the prompt payment of taxes and any other obligations, and to restore to income such reserves as may be unused; to use administration expenses and deductions for Estate or Income Tax purposes and to select any optional valuation date for Estate Tax purposes as my said Personal Representative deems advisable and in general to deal with property of my estate as fully and freely as if my said Personal Representative was the owner thereof, and in the Personal Representative's discretion, to do any and all things necessary for the prompt administration of my estate. I request that the Probate Court require no bond of my said Personal Representative.

Should it be necessary for a representative of my estate to qualify in any jurisdiction wherein my Personal Representative named herein cannot or may not desire to qualify as such, then I appoint as Personal Representative in such foreign jurisdiction such person or corporation as may be designated by my said Personal Representative, and the Personal Representative so named, shall, without giving any bond or other security, have in such other jurisdiction all the rights, powers, privileges, discretions and duties conferred or imposed upon my said Personal Representative under the provisions of this Will.

Guardians. Let's start with minor children. Yes, they can inherit property, but they can't receive their inheritance until they are 18 (or attain the age of majority). Until that time, their property is held by their guardian. In your will, you can name the guardian for their "estate" (i.e., the property they inherit from you) and a guardian for their person (someone who can take them to a physician, sign permission slips to play football or go on band trips, and so forth). So you'll have to decide who is to serve as guardian of the property (the estate) and who is to server as guardian of the person. The guardian of the estate controls the money; the guardian of the person is responsible for the physical welfare of your minor child, that is, the person who raises your child until adulthood. The Court may require the guardian to post a fidelity bond (which is an insurance policy). If the guardian you select turns out to be a thief, the fidelity insurance company will restore the stolen property, and probably sue your guardian for its losses (and maybe try to send them to prison).

Parents are natural guardians, so you don't have to name your spouse in your will, as the person nominated to be the guardian for your children.

It is all right to name someone from out of state, but don't name someone who is from another country, or is not a U.S. citizen. Name someone who has the same value system you do, but don't name felons or sex offenders. Courts will do background checks on the person you nominate as a guardian.

Once a guardian has been appointed, that person will report to the Court on a periodic basis, on how much money has been collected and spent in the child's behalf.

Here is sample language that might be used in your will:

> **Appointment of Guardian of Person.** In the event that my spouse, _____, shall predecease me, or both of us die in a common disaster, I direct that the exclusive care, custody and education of any named beneficiary, under age 18 or under disability (legal or otherwise), and any of my children born or adopted in the future, be entrusted as Guardian of the Person, during such periods of disability, to _____, of _____, to serve without bond.

> **Appointment of Guardian of the Property (Estate).** In the event that my spouse, _____, shall predecease me, or both of us die in a common disaster, I direct that the exclusive care, custody and education of any named beneficiary, under age 18 or under disability (legal or otherwise), and any of my children born or adopted in the future, be entrusted as Guardian of the Estate (property) , during such periods of disability, to _____, of _____, to serve without bond.

Debts, Taxes and Other Issues. You should also give instructions on how your debts are to be paid, who pays taxes (if there are any), whether certain people (normally minor children) can have use of their inheritance before reaching age 18 (through the use of a testamentary trust), and you can even create sub-trusts, so as to save some federal estate taxes. All of these topics will be covered later on, in more detail.

But the point is this: you can load your will up with valuable information. Keep in mind, however, that your will doesn't control everything you own (such as IRA beneficiaries).

Here's an example of what a will can say, relating to debts and taxes.

> My Personal Representative shall pay expenses of my last illness and funeral costs, claims, costs of administration and taxes assessed or associated by reason of my death. Any other debts secured in any way, not yet due, or payable in installments, may be postponed, extended or paid according to the terms of such indebtedness, and my estate may be closed and property be distributed subject to unpaid indebtedness and encumbrances.

> All estate, inheritance, legacy, succession or transfer taxes (including any interest and penalties thereon) imposed with respect to all property taxable by reason of my death, shall be paid by my Personal Representative, but each non-charitable beneficiary shall be chargeable (by my Personal Representative) with all inheritance, succession, transfer or estate taxes based upon the value such beneficiary's share bears to the value of the entire estate. My Personal Representative shall make such elections under the tax laws as the Personal Representative deems advisable, without regard to the relative interests of the beneficiaries. No election so made shall be subject to question by any beneficiary, and no adjustment shall be made between principal and income or in the relative interests of the beneficiaries to compensate for the effect of elections under the tax laws made by my Personal Representative.

Distribution of Estate. You may make gifts of property to people (please, no gifts to animals – this may be permitted by your state, but it is a fairly complicated topic – and no gifts to partnerships or corporations – gifts to non-profit and charitable entities are acceptable). These types of gifts are specific gifts ("bequests").

Many of you think that you have to dispose of all of your property, on an item by item basis. That approach is tedious, and you might leave something out. The easiest thing for you, after you have listed all of the specific bequests, is name residuary beneficiaries of your estate, and state the fractional amounts each beneficiary is to receive (or you may use percentages).

If you place conditions on gifts – for example, "I leave one-third of my estate to my son, Slow Learner, providing he graduates from college" – you'll want to use a trust, which will be explained in the next section.

In addition, if you leave property to minor children, you might want to place that part of your estate in a testamentary trust (see next section).

If your estate is short and simple, here's an example:

> If any person named below predeceases me, the gift to that person shall lapse. Providing the person(s) named below is/are living at the time of my decease, I give, devise and bequeath the following property to:
>
> Property described as follows: _____, to be distributed to
>
> _____
>
> If any person named below predeceases me, the gift to that person shall lapse. Providing the person(s) named below is/are living at the time of my decease, I give, devise and bequeath the following property to:
>
> Property described as follows: _____, to be distributed to
>
> _____
>
> If any person named below predeceases me, the gift to that person shall lapse. Providing the person(s) named below is/are living at the time of my decease, I give, devise and bequeath the following sum(s) to:
>
> $_____, to be distributed to _____

I give, devise and bequeath the rest, remainder and residue of my estate to my spouse, _____. If _____ predeceases me, the rest, remainder and residue of my estate shall be distributed as follows:

Beneficiary	Fractional Amount or Percentage
_____ if living, or if deceased, to his or her issue, per stirpes	___ %
_____ if living, or if deceased, to his or her issue, per stirpes	___ %
Total:	100%

Per Stirpes has nothing to do with stirrups (the metal frame where you slip your boots on a saddle). Per stirpes is a Latin phrase which means, "per branch". In a will it means that if a child dies before you, that child's share is split into equal shares for further distribution to his or her children.

Trusts. To simplify the concept, there are two types of trusts: those you create before you die (these are known as inter vivos (sometimes spelled "Intervivos") trusts, also known as Loving Trusts, Living Trusts, Declaration of Trust, or Trusts. This book deals with wills, so we won't explain Intervivos trusts, except to say that trusts are agreements you normally make with yourself (sometimes called "self settled" trusts). You create the trust (you are the trustor, grantor, trust maker, or settlor), and you deliver property to the trustee (you are normally the trustee). The trustee holds the property for the benefit of the beneficiary (normally, you are the beneficiary). When the settlor dies (that's you), the person you named as successor trustee takes over ownership of whatever property is left in the trust, and distributes the property to beneficiaries (whom you have named to inherit the property, after you die). There is no probate for property held in an inter vivos trust; thus, there is a savings of time and expense (no judges, and usually, not much time spent by a lawyer, who will help the successor trustee distribute the property).

There are several types of trusts you can create, and you can even create a trust within a will, known as a "testamentary trust". Since it does not come into effect until you die, there is no transfer of property to a trustee beforehand (as there is in an inter vivos trust). Though your will must go through the probate process, part (or all) of your estate will wind up in the hands of a trustee (usually a human being, but sometimes a trust company – that is, a corporation which has "trust powers", meaning, a corporation with a large net worth, which is usually regulated by the banking industry or other state agency; only "approved" corporations can exercise "trust powers").

If your will contains a testamentary trust, the trustee you select will own property, not for itself, but for the beneficiary or beneficiaries of the trust. The beneficiary may be a minor child, or someone under legal disability, or someone who doesn't get to inherit until age 25 (or whatever age you specify).

You will decide how the trustee disposes of the trust property. For example, the trustee may be given discretion to take part of the trust property (whether income or principal) and distribute it to a beneficiary, for education, support, maintenance, and so forth. At some point in time, however, the trust must come to an end, and the trustee must distribute the trust estate to a designated beneficiary.

In some states, the Trustee will file reports about its activities with the probate court (these reports are in the nature of financial statements). The trust beneficiaries can object to the reports, and the court will issue orders, which approve or disapprove of what the Trustee has done. In other states, no reports are required to be filed with the court, but the Trustee is expected to give an annual report to each beneficiary of the trust.

Examples are helpful, so take a look at this sample testamentary trust:

TRUST FOR CERTAIN BENEFICIARIES

6.1 *Trust for Persons Under Twenty-five Years of Age*. Notwithstanding any provision herein to the contrary, if any person who inherits any part of my estate hereunder is at the time of distribution under the age of twenty five years, I hereby create a testamentary trust, known as the Cracking Family Trust. The beneficiary who is under age twenty-five is a vested beneficiary, but my personal representative shall distribute such share to First Bank of Springfield, Illinois, which is the Trustee of this trust. The Trustee is to serve without bond, and shall receive all property delivered to the Trustee by the Personal Representative of my estate. A trust account shall be established for each beneficiary under age 25, and the Trustee shall separately administer such share for the beneficiary until he or she becomes 25 years of age, whereupon that share, and any accumulated income, shall be distributed to him or to her. The Trustee may use and distribute so much of the income, in its sole discretion, as is reasonably necessary or desirable for the support, health, general welfare, and education of such beneficiary; in addition, the Trustee may, in the Trustee's sole and absolute discretion, use and distribute the principal for any emergency or extraordinary medical need of the beneficiary. In carrying out each such trust, the Trustee may, in its sole discretion, make payments or distribution of income and principal: (a) directly to the beneficiary; (b) to the legal guardian of the person or estate, Trustee, or near relative of the beneficiary; and (c) to third persons for the support, education, welfare, or benefit of the beneficiary.

6.2 *Mandatory Termination of Trusts to Comply With Rule Against Perpetuities*. Any trust created under Section 6.1 shall finally terminate upon the distribution of all assets of such trust, and notwithstanding any other provision herein to the contrary, each such trust shall terminate so as not to violate the Rule Against Perpetuities. The Trustee shall take such actions as are required to terminate the trust, so that rule against perpetuities will not be violated.

6.3 *Termination of Small Trusts*. If any trust created by this Will should at any time become so small that in the opinion of the Trustee it cannot be efficiently and economically administered, the Trustee may, in the Trustee's sole discretion, terminate said trust and distribute any assets thereof to the beneficiaries entitled thereto, or as otherwise provided in Section 6.1.

6.4 *Spendthrift Trusts*. The interests of all individual beneficiaries in the corpus or income of any trust created herein are spendthrift trusts and shall not be subject to assignment, sale, mortgage, pledge, any voluntary or involuntary alienation, garnishment, attachments, execution, or process of court, nor be liable for the debts, contracts, torts or liabilities of any beneficiary.

6.5 *Other Provisions*

6.5.1. In the event any provision of this trust conflicts with any applicable state law (in existence now, or which may be enacted hereinafter, including without limitation, the Uniform Trust Code), the provisions of this instrument shall prevail.

6.5.2. If this trust contains any spendthrift provisions, then I declare that such spendthrift provisions constitute a material purpose of this trust.

6.5.3. No bond shall be required of any trustee serving hereunder.

6.5.4. If the trustee is an individual who becomes incapacitated, as determined by the trustee's physician, or if there is no such physician, then by two independent physicians, the incapacitated trustee shall no longer be qualified to serve in the office of trustee; in such event, the trustee who is designated as a successor trustee, under the terms of this trust, shall become the trustee, and assume the office of trustee. There is no requirement that such incapacity be determined by a Court proceeding.

6.5.5. If any beneficiary's former spouse attempts by court proceeding or otherwise, to attach such distributions, for any purpose, including, without limitation, unpaid support alimony (or rehabilitative alimony), then, in such event, such distributions shall be regarded as being discretionary distributions, which shall not be subject to attachment.

6.5.6. For purposes of this trust, a "qualified beneficiary" is a vested (not contingent) beneficiary who is entitled to receive present (not future) income or principal distributions; the definition of a qualified beneficiary does not include (and specifically excludes) any contingent beneficiary or any vested remainder beneficiary.

6.5.7. If the Trustee is granted discretion in making distributions to any beneficiary, such as, distributions for the beneficiary's health, education, support, or general welfare, the standards (or factors) to be used in determining whether any distribution is to be made, or the amount of any distribution, include the beneficiary's income and other financial resources, the beneficiary's spending habits, the beneficiary's accustomed standard of living, the beneficiary's financial acumen, the beneficiary's credit worthiness and stature (and credit report), the beneficiary's immediate and long term needs (including any extraordinary health need, including the procuring of health insurance), the beneficiary's intended use for the cash or property distributed from the trust estate, the beneficiary's academic record, the beneficiary's susceptibility to substance abuse, and the beneficiary's employment history.

The Trustee may deny distributions, based on one or a combination of these factors, or may make distributions, based on one or a combination of these factors. Once such a decision is made by the Trustee, such decision shall be regarded as being made in the sole and absolute discretion of the Trustee.

6.5.8. To the extent required, the Trustee may create a special needs trust for the benefit of any vested beneficiary hereunder, should the provisions made for such beneficiary hereunder make him or her ineligible for government benefits. The Trustee shall take all steps as are necessary or desirable in order to protect the rights of the beneficiary, but at the same time, not impair such beneficiary's receipt of government benefits, due to disability.

ARTICLE 7

ADMINISTRATIVE PROVISIONS FOR ALL TRUSTS

7.1 *Immediate Appointment of Trustees*. My personal representative shall immediately after the proving of my Will appoint as Trustee the person or corporation designated in this Will. The Trustee shall serve without bond. Immediately upon such appointment, the Trustee shall be deemed qualified without the need for court approval and shall immediately collect, and shall hold and administer under the applicable provisions hereof any insurance proceeds payable to the Trustee and any other funds or property when distributed to such Trustee.

7.2 *Powers of Trustees*. In the administration of the respective trusts, the Trustee shall exercise all powers conferred by all laws in effect at my death, and in addition to and not in modification or limitation of all powers conferred by law, the Trustee is hereby fully and completely empowered and authorized to sell, convey, and transfer all the trust assets, including real estate, to invest and reinvest the same with the broadest investment powers and discretion, and without being limited to trust investments as may be provided by law. My Trustee is hereby given full power and authority to operate and manage any business, property or investment, to vote stock, to retain unproductive or wasting assets, to compromise and settle claims, to purchase or sell trust assets from or to any other trust for a fair consideration, to lease for periods extending beyond the term of the trust, to commingle trust assets with assets of other trusts or in pooled investments or otherwise, to obtain advice and counsel for fees regarding investments, to delegate responsibility for investments to investment counselors for fees, and to do all things in connection with the respective trust estate, or any part thereof, which the said Trustee, in the exercise of his uncontrolled discretion, deems necessary and most beneficial in the best interests of the trust estates; and generally, to do any lawful act in relation to such trust property which the absolute owner thereof might do. The Trustee shall use good judgment in exercising the powers, discretion, and rights conferred by this trust and in performing duties as Trustee which are imposed by law, and, in order to feel free in doing so, the Trustee shall be exempt from liability for any action taken or omitted in good faith. However, the Trustee is not permitted to use any trust assets to pay for attorney's fees to any person or institution other than the trustee.

7.3 *Reliance on Trustee's Authority.* No person, firm, nor corporation dealing with the Trustee with reference to any of the trust property, if acting in good faith, shall be required to ascertain the authority of the Trustee nor to see to the performance of the trust, nor be responsible in any way for the proper application of funds or properties paid or delivered to the Trustee for the account of the trust but, if acting in good faith, may deal with the Trustee as though the Trustee were the unconditional owner.

7.4 *Prudent Man Investment Rule.* The Trustee may invest in any property in which an individual may make investments. In purchasing investments, the Trustee shall endeavor to exercise the judgment and care, in the circumstances then prevailing, which men of prudence, discretion, and intelligence exercise in the management of their own affairs, not in regard to speculation, but in regard to the permanent disposition of their funds, considering the probable safety of their capital. The trustee is not required to comply with the provisions of the Uniform Prudent Investors Act.

7.5 *Miscellaneous.* In the event any beneficiary (or contingent beneficiary) contests the provisions of this Trust as to its validity, other than matters dealing with the Trustee's administrative, contractual and statutory duties and responsibilities herein, the Trustee shall reduce the distribution to any such contesting beneficiary to $10.00, and distribute the remaining balance of such beneficiary's original share to the other beneficiaries, on a prorated basis (calculated using the percentages or fractions set forth hereinabove). Paragraph headings are used for convenience in locating various portions of this testamentary trust, and are not to be used in interpreting the verbiage and meaning of the trust.

7.6. *Additional Instructions.* For periods and purposes as the Trustee in its sole discretion may deem advisable, to employ attorneys, banks, brokers, custodians, investment counsel, investment advisors, specialists, bookkeepers, clerks, stenographers and other assistants and other agents, and without limitation as to specific purposes set forth hereinafter and herein, permitting such persons to perform any act or acts related to the trust, the trustee, defense of the trustee, defense of the trust instrument or defense of the trust estate, or acts relating to the beneficiaries, acts of administration, and the like, all during the Trustee's term of office. The Trustee has the power to delegate to them duties, rights and powers of the Trustee, including without limitation, including the right to vote on shares of stock constituting a part or all of the trust property, to grant a power of attorney, to exercise discretionary investment powers, or to grant a proxy. The Trustee is also granted the power to pay them for their services and reimburse their expenses from the trust estate. Under no circumstance, however, shall the trust estate, or the Trustee, pay for any attorneys fees for services rendered to anyone except the Trustee. The Trustee may invest in any property in which an individual may make investments.

There's a lot of verbiage in a trust. And trustees have a lot of "power" (discretion) over how property is distributed to a beneficiary. If your state has adopted the Uniform Trust Code the powers granted the trustee are much more extensive than what is listed in the sample.

Note there are provisions dealing with the Rule Against Perpetuities. This rule (we'll abbreviate it as RAP, which doesn't mean a form of music) limits how long a trust can last. If the trust lasts too long and violates the RAP, the trust is void. The easiest way to mend that problem is to state the trust will be terminated before it violates the RAP.

In the trust sample we have given, we haven't used a lot of imagination in creating conditions to be met before a beneficiary is entitled to inherit his or her share of the trust. But let's give an example that seems to be popular in some circles: testing a child for drugs. If you don't want a child to inherit unless he or she is drug-free, then consider the following language:

1. No distribution shall be made to my son, Joes O. N. Cracking, unless he is drug free. Joes O. N. Cracking should NOT be informed of the following drug testing schedule(s), until notified by the drug testing laboratory to provide a urine specimen. If he does not arrive at the laboratory within the allowed time, (2 hours after he's notified to provide the sample), that his absence will be considered a failure to comply, thus treated as a positive test for drugs present in his body.

2. The following schedule should be followed by the testing laboratory in order to ensure Joes O. N. Cracking is free of illegal drugs or alcohol.

   1) Joes should be tested the 51st, 52nd and 53rd days after he was first notified the testing would take place. If he is found to be free and clear of any illegal drugs or alcohol after these three (3) consecutive tests, he should be given his portion of the Trust.

   2) However, if these first tests reveal he has illegal controlled substance(s) or alcohol in his system, he should given a second chance to stop using drugs. Therefore, he should be given an additional 30-days to stop using drugs to ensure his body will be clean of any illegal drugs or alcohol. In addition, he should be informed that he will again be drug tested any time after an additional 30-day period. He shall be tested again on the 60th, 62nd and 63rd days from the last time he was tested. If he is found to be free and clear of any drugs/alcohol after these three tests he should be given his portion of the Cracking Family Trust. However, if any of these tests reveal any illegal controlled substances alcohol in his system he will forfeit his share of the Trust. Thus, his share of the Trust will be divided equally among the other beneficiaries of "The Cracking Family Trust."

Should you decide to create complicated conditions in a testamentary trust, read it over several times, to make certain it makes sense. I know you don't want to pay a lawyer to do this for you, but maybe you can negotiate a fee that is less than his or her normal fee. Remember, lawyers and judges don't think like you do, and rightly or wrongly, they hold the keys to the probate system. If you use a lawyer to do this for you, try to pick one that specializes in estate planning.

What wills don't control. Keep in mind that your will doesn't control everything you own. Here are some things to consider:

Rule 1: Wills don't control everything you own when you die.

Rule 2: IRAs, 401ks, 403bs, tax deferred annuities, life insurance policies, Section 457 plans, and the like, are paid to whomever you have named as a death beneficiary. Let's say you name Aunt Alice as the death beneficiary of your IRA. When you die, Aunt Alice gets whatever remains in your IRA, regardless of what's said in your will. But what if Aunt Alice dies first? The money is then paid to the contingent beneficiary you have named on your IRA. Suppose you forgot to designate a contingent beneficiary? Then the money is paid to "your estate" (and that goes through probate).

Rule 2A: So, exactly who is "my estate?" It is whomever you have named in your will as the residuary beneficiary (and if you don't have a will, then the money is paid to the people your state legislature thinks you wanted to receive your estate; this is defined in the Statute of Descent and Distribution – each state has a different statute).

Rule 3: If you own real estate or a bank account, as a joint tenant with right of survivorship, whoever survives you as a joint tenant inherits the property (there can be several joint tenants). Your will doesn't trump joint tenancy property. If one of the joint tenants predeceases you and THEN you die, then you revert to Rule 2A, and your heirs probably have a mess on their hands.

Rule 4: Wills don't control stock brokerage or money market accounts which have a TOD (transfer on death) designation, nor do wills control bank accounts which have a POD (pay on death) designation (some states have passed laws permitting TOD designations on deeds, and that deals with real estate; these are also called beneficiary deeds). But don't forget Rule 2A: if the person you name dies first, then your heirs might have the proverbial mess on their hands.

Rule 5: Some assets, such as cars, and intangible property (such as a bank account) can be transferred to heirs without probate. This procedure varies from state to state, and there are usually dollar limitations on what can be transferred without probate ($5,000 - $50,000). If the heir claiming the property isn't the residuary beneficiary under the will, the will might have to go through probate, to resolve the dispute.

Rule 6: Community property states (i.e., Texas, Louisiana, New Mexico, Colorado, Wisconsin, Arizona, Idaho, Nevada and Washington) let you distribute only half of your community property in your will, and your spouse might even have rights to a portion of your community property. Your will only controls what you own, which doesn't include the half interest owned by your spouse.

In a community property state you can devise (that means give) your separate property, without spousal interference (separate property includes what you owned before you got married, and property you inherited, which you didn't mix with your community property, viz., a joint bank account with your spouse).

Rule 7: Your will can't control restricted land (meaning, you are an enrolled Native American, and the land you own might be inalienable – OK, we'll try not to use big words – the land might not be transferable, unless the transfer is approved by the Bureau of Indian Affairs, or the Native American Tribe, such as, the Osage Nation, Cherokee Nation, etc.)

Rule 8: Property held in trust. Intervivos trusts will probably be dealt with in other books (certainly not this one, except for what's already been said), but here's the skinny: a trust is an agreement you make with a trustee (you may be the trustee, or you could be co-trustee with someone else). Property is transferred to the trustee(s), and the trustee(s) hold the property for the benefit of the beneficiary. When the trustee dies, a successor trustee takes over, and continues to hold the property for the benefit of the beneficiary. When a beneficiary dies, the next named beneficiary receives benefits. Sooner or later, the trust ends (the trust itself will normally explain how this works), and the trust property will be distributed to the beneficiaries.

We've said this before, but remember, there are two types of trust: those that take place when you die (called testamentary trusts; they are part of your last will and testament, thus, "testamentary"), and those that take place while you are alive (intervivos trusts, living trusts, etc.). Normally, trusts are revocable, but sometimes they aren't (meaning, they can't be changed; those are irrevocable trusts).

As mentioned in an earlier section, if you have a testamentary trust, your will controls the terms of the trust. If you have an intervivos trust, your will has no control over how the trust property is dealt with.

Rule 9: Premarital agreements (or prenuptial agreements). If you agree with your spouse as to how your estate is to be handled after the marriage has been consummated, in writing, you have made a prenuptial agreement. That prenuptial agreement might trump the provisions in your will. Much depends on what is contained in your prenuptial agreement.

What wills do control. Has the time come for a pop quiz on what's been covered? Hmmm. Not a good idea.

Maybe looking at these rules from a different angle will help. When you die, your will controls:

1. Property that is in your name alone (don't forget rule 7 in the preceding chapter, which deals with restricted land, which is part of the Native American rules; we won't mention this concept again – if the land is "restricted" because it is "Indian land", you may own the land in your name alone, but your will doesn't control the land, if you attempt to give the land to someone other than another enrolled Native American).

2. Property you own as a tenant in common with someone else (and you ask, what is a tenant in common?) A tenant in common is an old English concept, but you have to look at the deed to the real estate in question, to see how it is worded: generally, if the grantees – meaning, the ones who bought the property – are George Able and Ellen Able – with no other qualifying words or phrases, such as, "tenants by the entirety" or "joint tenants with right of survivorship" – then each owns an undivided one half interest in the land. When George dies, Ellen continues to own her undivided one half, but George's undivided one-half doesn't pass to Ellen, it passes to his heirs (if he dies without a will) or to whomever he has named in his will. Another example: if you own an undivided $1/6^{th}$ interest in minerals, you own that $1/6^{th}$ interest as a tenant in common. When you die, this interest will go through the probate process (unless you have transferred your interest to an Intervivos trust, or unless you have filed a transfer on death deed with the county where the minerals are located).

3. Property that inadvertently winds up in your probate estate (for example, you forgot to name a death beneficiary on an IRA or insurance policy, or property you inherited and forgot to do a new deed which names your spouse as a joint tenant) is controlled by your will.

4. Property covered by a testamentary trust (which means, you own property in categories 1 – 3) is part of your probate estate, and is covered by your will.

Types of wills. There are two types of wills: handwritten (holographic, and in some states "olographic") or typed wills. Some states permit verbal (or oral) wills, which are also known as nun-cupative wills, but don't assume a court will enforce the provisions of a verbal will.

Not all states permit handwritten wills. Should you decide to do one of these, keep in mind that it needs to be in your handwriting, dated and signed by you. In most instances, you will probably not need witnesses or a notary public, but this book doesn't cover this type of will, because of the variations from state to state.

If the will you plan on signing is typed, you must nonetheless follow certain guidelines. You must have the legal capacity to sign a will, which means, you are over age 18, and are of sound mind and memory. The will must be witnessed by at least two persons (who should be disinterested, competent persons – an heir might lose an inheritance if the heir signs as a witness), and the witnesses must see you sign the will, and in most states, the witnesses must sign the will in your presence and the presence of the other witness. In all states, the witnesses will attest (this is a term of art) to the fact that they saw you sign the will, that you asked them to sign it, and that you declared that the document to be your last will and testament.

In addition, when you sign the will, you must do so voluntarily, meaning, you're not acting under fraud, duress or undue influence.

Husbands and wives are normally permitted to sign a single will, which is known as a mutual and conjoint will. When one spouse dies, the other spouse cannot change the terms of the will at a later date (the will becomes irrevocable). Some states do not permit mutual and conjoint wills.

Capacity. When you sign a will, you must have testamentary capacity. If you don't have testamentary capacity, your will is invalid.

So exactly how do you prove that you have testamentary capacity? Part of the answer is in the verbiage used in the will – your will should state that you are of sound mind and memory. But if the will is to be admitted to probate, who is to say whether you had all of your marbles when you signed the will? The witnesses and notary public. They are adding credence that you are mentally "stable".

There are additional "tests" that help determine whether you have testamentary capacity. First, you need to know the bounty of your estate (meaning, you need to know what you own. Second, you also need to know who are the normal heirs of your estate (your spouse, children, and in some instances, parents, siblings, and so forth). It is advisable to put these names in your will (such an addition to your will indicates you know who your heirs are). If you have no spouse or children, you should construct a good family tree in the will.

Burial arrangements. When you die, your will is of no force and effect until it has been admitted to probate. This might take a month or longer, so the question is, should I mention burial arrangements in my will? You can do so, but it might be meaningless. Some states may give credence to a request in your will that you be cremated, or some other burial arrangement, but due to delays in the probate process, whatever request in your will might be mooted. If you want to be cremated, we suggest you make arrangements with the state cremation society.

Here is some suggested language on burial arrangements:

> I request that my remains (my body) be cremated.

Wrapping things up: Signing (executing) the Will.

Now that you have your will in order, let's review the formalities of getting it signed:

Rule 1: Each state has its own set of rules as to how a will must be signed. Follow the rules of your state (you may go to this website to look up the rules for your state; some of the state statutes are not as clear as others:
http://www.willcrafter.com/state_law_summary.xlsx).

Rule 2: You must sign the will in the presence of two witnesses, who cannot be related to you by birth or marriage, and in most instances, are not beneficiaries named under the will.

Some states permit "self authentication" of the will, which means, the will must be notarized. If you live in a state that permits that sort of thing (and most states do), then your witness will not have to show up in probate court after you die, and testify that (1) you identified the will as your will, (2) that you asked them to sign the will in your presence, and in the presence of the other witness, and (3) that you were of sound mind, memory, not under duress, undue influence, or were being defrauded when you signed the will.

Rule 3: Don't lose the original of the will, and please tell someone where it is located. The original will is needed after you die (photocopies are not admissible in probate court, in the majority of cases).

Rule 4: If you are using a DIY form from a source other than WillCrafter, check the verbiage in your state dealing with signature requirements (go to http://willcrafter.com/ state_law_summary.xlsx for the links to your state, and the applicable laws on signing your will.

Rule 5: Number the pages of your will.

Rule 6: In Louisiana, sign your name at the end of every page.

Here is an example of language Florida expects you to use, when you sign a will. This verbiage does you no good if you live in Nevada:

STATE OF FLORIDA
COUNTY OF OCALA

I, SALLY OLD MAUGH, declare to the officer taking my acknowledgment of this instrument, and to the subscribing witnesses, that I signed this instrument as my will.

_____
Testator/Testatrix

We, DICK DEADEYE and TWO EYED JACK, have been sworn by the officer signing below, and declare to that officer on our oaths that the testator/testatrix declared the instrument to be the testator/testatrix's will and signed it in our presence and that we each signed the instrument as a witness in the presence of the testator/testatrix and of each other.

_____
WITNESS

_____
ADDRESS OF WITNESS

_____
WITNESS

_____
ADDRESS OF WITNESS

Acknowledged and subscribed before me by the testator/testatrix, Sally Old Maugh, who is personally known to me or who has produced (state type of identification) ____ as identification, and sworn to and subscribed before me by the witnesses, Dick Deadeye who is personally known to me or who have produced (state type of identification) ____ as identification and Two Eyed Jack who is personally known to me or who has produced (state type of identification) ____ as identification, and subscribed by me in the presence of the testator/testarix and the subscribing witnesses, all on (date).

(Signed) _____

SEAL

_____

(Official Capacity of Officer)

Notice that the testatrix and witness have to sign twice. If you live in a state where self proved wills are not permitted, or in states that permit you to do so, you will only sign once. Ask the witnesses to print their names very clearly in the blank spaces, and when you sign the will, tell the witnesses and the notary that you are signing the document as your last will and testament, and that you are asking them to witness your signing, and asking them to sign in the presence of each other.

If you live in Louisiana, sign your name at the end of each page.

Comfort example, to use when comparing your DIY will with the following. Here is sample will, which you can review, and compare with what you have done for yourself (again, this is a Florida will, which won't help you if you are from Alaska).

Last Will and Testament
Of Sally O. Maugh

My name is Sally O. Maugh. I reside in Despot, Florida, and I am of sound mind and memory, and I desire to make proper provision for the distribution of my entire estate when I die. I hereby declare and publish this to be my Last Will and Testament, and I hereby revoke any and all Wills and codicils (amendments) I have previously made.

Article 1

Family Status. I declare that I am married . My spouse is George Maugh. I have three children, who are: George Maugh, Jr., Sally O. Maugh, Jr., and Unexpected Maugh. All are living.

Definitions. As used in this Will, the terms "child", "children", "issue", "lawful issue", "descendant", or "descendants", shall include persons legally adopted. Where applicable, references in this Will to the masculine shall include the feminine and to the singular shall include the plural.

Other matters. I have intentionally made no provision for any child born after the date of this will, and furthermore, have intentionally made no provision for any spouse not mentioned herein, or any spouse I may have at the time of my death, or any other person not mentioned. If any portion of this will is invalid, for any reason, the remainder of the will shall nonetheless be considered as a valid last will and testament. Should any part of my will be determined to be unenforceable, the other parts of the will are valid and enforceable.

Additionally, in the event any beneficiary (or contingent beneficiary or claimant) contests the provisions of this Will as to its validity, my capacity to make this Will, or any other aspect which might affect the distribution to such person (other than matters dealing with the Personal Representative's administrative and statutory duties and responsibilities herein), I direct the Personal Representative to reduce the distribution to any such contesting person to $1.00, and to distribute the remaining balance of such person's original share (if any) to the other beneficiaries, on a prorated basis.

Article 2

Appointment of Personal Representative and Successor. I nominate, constitute and appoint my spouse, George Maugh, as Personal Representative of my estate under this, my Last Will and Testament, to serve without bond. In the event that he/she should predecease me or shall be unable to serve, I then designate Local Trust Company as substitute or successor Personal Representatives. I request that the Probate Court require no bond of my Substitute or Successor Personal Representatives. My Personal Representative(s) shall (collectively) receive a fee of no more than 2.25% of my probate estate, plus reimbursement for out of pocket expenses and advances.

Powers of Personal Representative. My said Personal Representative shall have the power, in addition to and not in modification of all common law and statutory power, and without obtaining any Order or other approval of any Court to settle and adjust all claims and demands in favor of or against my estate; to defer payment of any claim or portion thereof that is not due and payable; to retain any property in the same form or instrument as that in which it is received; to invest or reinvest principal and income in such securities or other property, real or personal as my said Personal Representative may deem advisable, without being limited to investments which fiduciaries are authorized by law to make; to determine whether money or property shall be considered income or principal or partly income and partly principal; to charge or apportion expenses and losses to principal or income as my said Personal Representative deems just and equitable; to manage, control, maintain, improve, lease for any term, rent, exchange, sell, convey and transfer at public or private sale, all or any part of the real or personal property comprising my estate, for such prices and upon such terms as my said Personal Representative deems advisable, and to execute and deliver proper instruments of conveyance and transfer; to execute and deliver proxies, powers of attorney and such other instruments as are incident to the holding, control and voting of corporate securities or the sale or exchange thereof; to borrow money and to execute promissory notes and use any property of my estate as security therefor; to make any division or distribution in money, in kind, or partly in each, and in making any such division or interest therein, to any person, although different in kind from property allocated or distributed to any other person; to create such reserves out of income as such Personal Representative deems advisable for depreciation, obsolescence, amortization and to insure the prompt payment of taxes and any other obligations, and to restore to income such reserves as may be unused; to use administration expenses and deductions for Estate or Income Tax purposes and to select any optional valuation date for Estate Tax purposes as my said Personal Representative deems advisable and in general to deal with property of my estate as fully and freely as if my said Personal Representative was the owner thereof, and in the Personal Representative's discretion, to do any and all things necessary for the prompt administration of my estate. I request that the Probate Court require no bond of my said Personal Representative.

Should it be necessary for a representative of my estate to qualify in any jurisdiction wherein my Personal Representative named herein cannot or may not desire to qualify as such, then I appoint as Personal Representative in such foreign jurisdiction such person or corporation as may be designated by my said Personal Representative, and the Personal Representative so named, shall, without giving any bond or other security, have in such other jurisdiction all the rights, powers, privileges, discretions and duties conferred or imposed upon my said Personal Representative under the provisions of this Will.

Article 3

Appointment of Guardian of Person. In the event that my spouse, George Maugh, shall predecease me, or both of us die in a common disaster, I direct that the exclusive care, custody and education of any named beneficiary, under age 18 or under disability (legal or otherwise), and any of my children born or adopted in the future, be entrusted as Guardian of the Person, during such periods of disability, to George Maugh, Jr. of Lexington, Kentucky, to serve without bond.

Appointment of Guardian of the Property (Estate). In the event that my spouse, George Maugh shall predecease me, or both of us die in a common disaster, I direct that the exclusive care, custody and education of any named beneficiary, under age 18 or under disability (legal or otherwise), and any of my children born or adopted in the future, be entrusted as Guardian of the Estate (property) during such periods of disability, to Local Trust Company of Tampa, Florida, to serve without bond.

Article 4

My Personal Representative (also known as Independent Executor or Executor) shall pay expenses of my last illness and funeral costs, claims, costs of administration and taxes assessed by reason of my death. Any other debts secured in any way, not yet due, or payable in installments, may be postponed, extended or paid according to the terms of such indebtedness, and my estate may be closed and property be distributed subject to unpaid indebtedness and encumbrances.

All estate, inheritance, legacy, succession or transfer taxes (including any interest and penalties thereon) imposed with respect to all property taxable by reason of my death, shall be paid by my Personal Representative, but each beneficiary shall be chargeable (by my Personal Representative) with all inheritance, succession, transfer or estate taxes based upon the value such beneficiary's share bears to the value of the entire estate. My Personal Representative shall make such elections under the tax laws as the Personal Representative deems advisable, without regard to the relative interests of the beneficiaries. No election so made shall be subject to question by any beneficiary, and no adjustment shall be made between principal and income or in the relative interests of the beneficiaries to compensate for the effect of elections under the tax laws made by my Personal Representative.

Article 5

5.1   If any person named below predeceases me, the gift to that person shall lapse. Providing the person(s) named below is/are living at the time of my decease, I give, devise and bequeath the following property to:

Property described as follows:
    Jewelry, to be distributed to Sally O. Maugh, Jr.
    Piano, to George Maugh, Jr.

5.2   I give, devise and bequeath the rest, remainder and residue of my estate to my spouse, George Maugh.

If George Maugh predeceases me, the rest, remainder and residue of my estate shall be distributed as follows:

Beneficiary	Fractional Amount or Percentage
George Maugh, Jr. if living, or if deceased, to his issue, per stirpes	1/3
Sally O. Maugh, Jr. if living, or if deceased, to her issue, per stirpes	1/3
Unexpected Maugh, if living, or if deceased, to his issue, per stirpes	1/3

Article 6

TRUST FOR CERTAIN BENEFICIARIES

6.1 *Trust for Persons Under Twenty-five Years of Age.* Notwithstanding any provision herein to the contrary, if any person who inherits any part of my estate hereunder is at the time of distribution under the age of twenty five years, I hereby create a testamentary trust, known as the Cracking Family Trust. The beneficiary who is under age twenty-five is a vested beneficiary, but my personal representative shall distribute such share to First Bank of Springfield, Illinois, which is the Trustee of this trust. The Trustee is to serve without bond, and shall receive all property delivered to the Trustee by the Personal Representative of my estate. A trust account shall be established for each beneficiary under age 25, and the Trustee shall separately administer such share for the beneficiary until he or she becomes 25 years of age, whereupon that share, and any accumulated income, shall be distributed to him or to her. The Trustee may use and distribute so much of the income, in its sole discretion, as is reasonably necessary or desirable for the support, health, general welfare, and education of such beneficiary; in addition, the Trustee may, in the Trustee's sole and absolute discretion, use and distribute the principal for any emergency or extraordinary medical need of the beneficiary. In carrying out each such trust, the Trustee may, in its sole discretion, make payments or distribution of income and principal: (a) directly to the beneficiary; (b) to the legal guardian of the person or estate, Trustee, or near relative of the beneficiary; and (c) to third persons for the support, education, welfare, or benefit of the beneficiary.

6.2 *Mandatory Termination of Trusts to Comply With Rule Against Perpetuities.* Any trust created under Section 6.1 shall finally terminate upon the distribution of all assets of such trust, and notwithstanding any other provision herein to the contrary, each such trust shall terminate so as not to violate the Rule Against Perpetuities. The Trustee shall take such actions as are required to terminate the trust, so that rule against perpetuities will not be violated.

6.3 *Termination of Small Trusts.* If any trust created by this Will should at any time become so small that in the opinion of the Trustee it cannot be efficiently and economically administered, the Trustee may, in the Trustee's sole discretion, terminate said trust and distribute any assets thereof to the beneficiaries entitled thereto, or as otherwise provided in Section 6.1.

6.4 *Spendthrift Trusts.* The interests of all individual beneficiaries in the corpus or income of any trust created herein are spendthrift trusts and shall not be subject to assignment, sale, mortgage, pledge, any voluntary or involuntary alienation, garnishment, attachments, execution, or process of court, nor be liable for the debts, contracts, torts or liabilities of any beneficiary.

6.5 Other Provisions

6.5.1. In the event any provision of this trust conflicts with any applicable state law (in existence now, or which may be enacted hereinafter, including without limitation, the Uniform Trust Code), the provisions of this instrument shall prevail.

6.5.2. If this trust contains any spendthrift provisions, then I declare that such spendthrift provisions constitute a material purpose of this trust.

6.5.3. No bond shall be required of any trustee serving hereunder.

6.5.4. If the trustee is an individual who becomes incapacitated, as determined by the trustee's physician, or if there is no such physician, then by two independent physicians, the incapacitated trustee shall no longer be qualified to serve in the office of trustee; in such event, the trustee who is designated as a successor trustee, under the terms of this trust, shall become the trustee, and assume the office of trustee. There is no requirement that such incapacity be determined by a Court proceeding.

6.5.5. If any beneficiary's former spouse attempts by court proceeding or otherwise, to attach such distributions, for any purpose, including, without limitation, unpaid support alimony (or rehabilitative alimony), then, in such event, such distributions shall be regarded as being discretionary distributions, which shall not be subject to attachment.

6.5.6. For purposes of this trust, a "qualified beneficiary" is a vested (not contingent) beneficiary who is entitled to receive present (not future) income or principal distributions; the definition of a qualified beneficiary does not include (and specifically excludes) any contingent beneficiary or any vested remainder beneficiary.

6.5.7. If the Trustee is granted discretion in making distributions to any beneficiary, such as, distributions for the beneficiary's health, education, support, or general welfare, the standards (or factors) to be used in determining whether any distribution is to be made, or the amount of any distribution, include the beneficiary's income and other financial resources, the beneficiary's spending habits, the beneficiary's accustomed standard of living, the beneficiary's financial acumen, the beneficiary's credit worthiness and stature (and credit report), the beneficiary's immediate and long term needs (including any extraordinary health need, including the procuring of health insurance), the beneficiary's intended use for the cash or property distributed from the trust estate, the beneficiary's academic record, the beneficiary's susceptibility to substance abuse, and the beneficiary's employment history.

The Trustee may deny distributions, based on one or a combination of these factors, or may make distributions, based on one or a combination of these factors. Once such a decision is made by the Trustee, such decision shall be regarded as being made in the sole and absolute discretion of the Trustee.

6.5.8. To the extent required, the Trustee may create a special needs trust for the benefit of any vested beneficiary hereunder, should the provisions made for such beneficiary hereunder make him or her ineligible for government benefits. The Trustee shall take all steps as are necessary or desirable in order to protect the rights of the beneficiary, but at the same time, not impair such beneficiary's receipt of government benefits, due to disability.

ARTICLE 7

ADMINISTRATIVE PROVISIONS FOR ALL TRUSTS

7.1 Immediate Appointment of Trustees. My personal representative shall immediately after the proving of my Will appoint as Trustee the person or corporation designated in this Will. The Trustee shall serve without bond. Immediately upon such appointment, the Trustee shall be deemed qualified without the need for court approval and shall immediately collect, and shall hold and administer under the applicable provisions hereof any insurance proceeds payable to the Trustee and any other funds or property when distributed to such Trustee.

7.2 Powers of Trustees. In the administration of the respective trusts, the Trustee shall exercise all powers conferred by all laws in effect at my death, and in addition to and not in modification or limitation of all powers conferred by law, the Trustee is hereby fully and completely empowered and authorized to sell, convey, and transfer all the trust assets, including real estate, to invest and reinvest the same with the broadest investment powers and discretion, and without being limited to trust investments as may be provided by law. My Trustee is hereby given full power and authority to operate and manage any business, property or investment, to vote stock, to retain unproductive or wasting assets, to compromise and settle claims, to purchase or sell trust assets from or to any other trust for a fair consideration, to lease for periods extending beyond the term of the trust, to commingle trust assets with assets of other trusts or in pooled investments or otherwise, to obtain advice and counsel for fees regarding investments, to delegate responsibility for investments to investment counselors for fees, and to do all things in connection with the respective trust estate, or any part thereof, which the said Trustee, in the exercise of his uncontrolled discretion, deems necessary and most beneficial in the best interests of the trust estates; and generally, to do any lawful act in relation to such trust property which the absolute owner thereof might do. The Trustee shall use good judgment in exercising the powers, discretion, and rights conferred by this trust and in performing duties as Trustee which are imposed by law, and, in order to feel free in doing so, the Trustee shall be exempt from liability for any action taken or omitted in good faith. However, the Trustee is not permitted to use any trust assets to pay for attorney's fees to any person or institution other than the trustee.

7.3 Reliance on Trustee's Authority. No person, firm, nor corporation dealing with the Trustee with reference to any of the trust property, if acting in good faith, shall be required to ascertain the authority of the Trustee nor to see to the performance of the trust, nor be responsible in any way for the proper application of funds or properties paid or delivered to the Trustee for the account of the trust but, if acting in good faith, may deal with the Trustee as though the Trustee were the unconditional owner.

7.4 Prudent Man Investment Rule. The Trustee may invest in any property in which an individual may make investments. In purchasing investments, the Trustee shall endeavor to exercise the judgment and care, in the circumstances then prevailing, which men of prudence, discretion, and intelligence exercise in the management of their own affairs, not in regard to speculation, but in regard to the permanent disposition of their funds, considering the probable safety of their capital. The trustee is not required to comply with the provisions of the Uniform Prudent Investors Act.

7.5 Miscellaneous. In the event any beneficiary (or contingent beneficiary) contests the provisions of this Trust as to its validity, other than matters dealing with the Trustee's administrative, contractual and statutory duties and responsibilities herein, the Trustee shall reduce the distribution to any such contesting beneficiary to $10.00, and distribute the remaining balance of such beneficiary's original share to the other beneficiaries, on a prorated basis (calculated using the percentages or fractions set forth hereinabove). Paragraph headings are used for convenience in locating various portions of this testamentary trust, and are not to be used in interpreting the verbiage and meaning of the trust.

7.6. Additional Instructions. For periods and purposes as the Trustee in its sole discretion may deem advisable, to employ attorneys, banks, brokers, custodians, investment counsel, investment advisors, specialists, bookkeepers, clerks, stenographers and other assistants and other agents, and without limitation as to specific purposes set forth hereinafter and herein, permitting such persons to perform any act or acts related to the trust, the trustee, defense of the trustee, defense of the trust instrument or defense of the trust estate, or acts relating to the beneficiaries, acts of administration, and the like, all during the Trustee's term of office. The Trustee has the power to delegate to them duties, rights and powers of the Trustee, including without limitation, including the right to vote on shares of stock constituting a part or all of the trust property, to grant a power of attorney, to exercise discretionary investment powers, or to grant a proxy. The Trustee is also granted the power to pay them for their services and reimburse their expenses from the trust estate. Under no circumstance, however, shall the trust estate, or the Trustee, pay for any attorneys fees for services rendered to anyone except the Trustee. The Trustee may invest in any property in which an individual may make investments.

STATE OF FLORIDA
COUNTY OF OCALA

I, SALLY OLD MAUGH, declare to the officer taking my acknowledgment of this instrument, and to the subscribing witnesses, that I signed this instrument as my will.

_____
Testator/Testatrix

We, DICK DEADEYE and TWO EYED JACK, have been sworn by the officer signing below, and declare to that officer on our oaths that the testator/testatrix declared the instrument to be the testator/testarix's will and signed it in our presence and that we each signed the instrument as a witness in the presence of the testator/testatrix and of each other.

_____
WITNESS

_____
ADDRESS OF WITNESS

_____
WITNESS

_____
ADDRESS OF WITNESS

Acknowledged and subscribed before me by the testator/testatrix, Sally Old Maugh, who is personally known to me or who has produced (state type of identification) _____ as identification, and sworn to and subscribed before me by the witnesses, Dick Deadeye who is personally known to me or who have produced (state type of identification) _____ as identification and Two Eyed Jack who is personally known to me or who has produced (state type of identification) _____ as identification, and subscribed by me in the presence of the testator/testarix and the subscribing witnesses, all on (date).

(Signed) _____
SEAL

_____
(Official Capacity of Officer)

Every state has its own rules on signing wills. Louisiana may be the odd man out, in the sense that every will must be signed by the testator/testatrix, at the bottom of every page. In addition to this quirk, each state has its own "mandated" language for attestation, and self proving wills (some states don't permit "self proving" wills), so care must be taken to insure that your will contains the right language.

Although WillCrafter and WillCrafter Lite have incorporated the signing rules for each state, you might have another DIY will program or app. To double check the language in your app, if you are inclined to do that sort of thing (and you ought to), go to this website and do some research for your state's requirements (some references are "incomplete"; the web address for each state may be found at http://www.willcrafter.com/state_law_summary.xlsx -- you may have to read several sections of the statutes to distill what each state requires).

Chapter 4: TAX SHELTERED TRUSTS

Tax sheltered trusts ("TST") are created in a will, or in a revocable trust. The purpose of these added provisions is to help heirs (other than husbands and wives) shelter the estate from some federal estate taxes. Most people won't be affected by federal estate taxes, because their taxable estates will be less than $5,000,000. This section of the book discusses estates over $5,000,000. If an estate is over $5 MM, the estate is taxed at a flat rate of 40%.

So what do tax sheltered trusts (TSTs) do? If properly implemented, TSTs double the amount of tax credit, if you are married. There is a related concept, known as the Portability Rule; this rule permits a married couple to use $10,000,000 worth of credits ($5,000,000 each), without creating a credit sheltered trust. If the spouses own properties in their own names, but in disproportionate amounts (e.g., the H owns $6,000,000 and the W owns $4,000,000). Under the portability rules, the spouses can "pool" their resources so as to achieve the full benefit of $10,000,000 exemptions from federal estate taxes. The portability rules are somewhat independent of the credit shelter rules, but no penalties attach if a couple doesn't have a credit sheltered trust.

Let's muddle through the mechanics of how credit sheltered trusts (or tax sheltered trusts) work.

Determine Net Worth First. The starting point begins with an assessment of your actual net worth. This assessment will also give you a fair indication of how much of your estate is potentially taxable. Once you know the size of your estate and the potential estate tax, you can take specific steps to eliminate tax in some cases, minimize it in others, and insure that there's money on hand to pay what's due.

The Gross Taxable Estate. For valuation purposes, your gross taxable estate includes every type of property you own "to the extent of your interest in it." For citizens and legal residents, this includes all property, wherever it's located. Also included is property that you may have disposed of legally, but have continued to control during your lifetime. And your gross taxable estate may include transfers of property with a retained life estate, transfers that take effect at death, transfers that are conditional on survivorship, and transfers made three years before death. Once you know whether your estate might be taxable, please take into account the "marital deduction" (next paragraph).

Marital Deduction. You can leave an unlimited amount of your estate to your spouse, free of federal estate tax. During your lifetime, you can make a gift to your spouse without any gift tax consequences. (There are restrictions on gifts to spouses who aren't US citizens, although careful planning can avoid many of these taxes.)

Death of First Spouse. Estate problems generally will not arise until your spouse dies. Then, unless you've planned ahead, anything you own over $5,000,000 (assuming you die in 2013) will be subject to progressively steep taxes.

With proper planning, you and your spouse can shelter as much as $5 million of property from federal estate taxes with a fairly simple device – a revocable living trust which has necessary language added to it. Using a revocable living trust with TST additions, you and your spouse can each pass along $5,000,000 free of federal estate taxes.

Here's an example of how to shelter your estate: First, divide your property equally between yourself and your spouse, with you and your spouse each owning $5,000,000 worth of property; you can accomplish such an allocation with a trust. If you can't divide the estate equally because you own IRAs, then a bit more planning is required, but the same results can be achieved.

Use of Trust During Your Lifetimes. Because the trust instrument is revocable – that is, you can change it – you will not have to file any additional tax returns. As a matter of fact, you will be able to use your property much the same way you now use it. The primary difference in owning property in trust is this – title to the property will be in the name of a trustee (for example, you will be the trustee, and what you own will be in the name of Sam Jones, Trustee – assuming your name is Sam Jones). You will still be able to use the property, just as you now do.

When one of you dies, one part of the trust (valued up to $5,000,000) will pay the other spouse income for life. The trust can also allow the surviving spouse to use the assets, if necessary.

Meantime, the surviving spouse also has the unlimited use of the other $5,000,000 during his or her lifetime. On the death of the surviving spouse, the money in both trusts would go to your beneficiaries (your children, for example), without any federal estate taxes (assuming there are $10,000,000 of assets when the surviving spouse dies).

One other word of caution: this article does not take into account state estate taxes, which may increase the total estate taxes.

FYI, the $5,000,000 in credits is indexed annually. For persons dying in 2013, the amount of the exemption is $5,250,000.

In summary, TSTs can lower estate taxes. But language must be added to the trust to wind up with an estate tax benefit.

Chapter 5: LONG TERM CARE

Though he did not elaborate on the topic, C. S. Lewis commented in a letter to a friend that he was having a difficult time in adjusting to the "planned economy" of Great Britain (the letter was penned circa 1930). Today we have taken for granted the "planned economy" in which we live, but we must remember that life has not always been as it is now. Stated differently, and from a historical perspective, every society from the beginning of civilization until now, has fostered some type of government interference with our private lives, and in so doing, gives us a "planned economy", which we must work through or around.

People have always had to bow to the king, whether it be in tilling the soil for him, harvesting crops, raising cattle, being drafted on the spot for naval service, or in paying taxes. In the United States, the "king", i.e., government, has now made us all a part of an economically planned community. One attribute of being part of an economically planned community deals with caring for the elderly. In times past, pneumonia routinely took the lives of the elderly, and society grieved the loss of its seniors – but prolonging the care of its elders was not a family or government issue. Times are now different. Medical science and pharmaceuticals have neutralized life-taking diseases such as pneumonia, and we live longer lives. Because our parents do not want to burden the children with their elder care needs, what solutions does our "planned economy" have in store for our parents and the elderly?

Simply put, how best can we care for mom and dad, when they cannot care for themselves? Though nursing homes have become the "answer" to the question, the costs associated with putting mom and dad in a nursing home is out of the reach of most families. If that is the case, does our government take over these expenses? Yes and no.

Let's begin with the economics involved, and start at the beginning, in 1965. Though the results were known before the legislation was passed, i.e., economic disaster for the national budget, during the Lyndon Johnson years, Congress adopted the Medicare program, which provided for health care benefits for those 65 and older. The program is paid for as part of our tax system, by Americans who earn wages (those who do not work, and who have passive or unearned income, might not have pay Medicare taxes). It is from this system that Medicaid programs began.

First, where does the government money come from? From every dollar of wages that is earned, employers send 15.3% of all wages paid to the Social Security Administration (and the U. S. Department of Treasury); half of the 15.3% is paid by the employee, half by the employer. Though Congress has not earmarked funds paid into the U. S. Treasury, in the sense that all funds received are placed in a common pool, here's what is to happen, theoretically: 12.9% of the 15.3% is used to pay for social security benefits, and 2.4% of the 15.3% is used to pay for all other benefit programs, including nursing home costs (but only for people who qualify for benefits, most of whom are over age 65).

The government then distributes the funds to the states, based on population (by and large), and the states administer how the funds are distributed. There are strings attached to the federal funds, and that is the primary topic addressed in this article.

Suppose mom or dad must be placed in a nursing home, and let's further assume they live in Ohio. If an aged Buckeye needs financial assistance to pay for nursing home bills, but has no financial resources, an Ohio health care agency (perhaps the

Ohio Department of Aging) will pay for those expenses, using Federal dollars it has received.

Now what strings are attached to these funds? Whoever is eligible for nursing home benefits loses certain rights to their property, which in effect, means the children will lose any chance of inheriting property from mom and dad.

So who is eligible for nursing home benefits? Obviously, not every elderly person in Ohio. Though each state establishes its own criteria for eligibility, these are the general requirements: a person cannot have too much wealth, nor can a person receive too much income. Unless a person is eligible under both criteria, the state will not pay the nursing home bills.

In most instances the local Department of Human Services office will provide a list of current eligibility rules. Currently, in most states, a person's income level cannot exceed much more than $2,200 per month (some states are classified as income cap states, as opposed to a "spend down" states). If income exceeds that amount, an exception might be made through the use of a Medicaid Income Trust (a Miller Trust, also called an Income Cap Trust or Qualified Income Trust). Second, a person cannot own much property (this varies, but the limits may be as low as $2,000 (or $27,000 for a married couple – however, certain property, generally referred to as excluded resources, are not always counted – for example, if the patient has the chance of returning to his or her home, then the home is not counted as a "resource", and is treated as an exempt asset or excluded resource). If the patient is married and his or her spouse is at home, that spouse can retain a fixed amount per month, which may be less than $3,000 a month. Computing these amounts depends on formulas, which requires a bit of analysis of income, living expenses and so forth, and is beyond the scope of this book. The amounts given in this paragraph change from year to year.

Suppose an elderly person qualifies for nursing home benefits, and stays in a nursing home for two years, then dies. What happens to the exempt resources? After the person dies, and the assets are being probated (including the exempt resources), the state will make a claim against the probate estate, and seek reimbursement for every dollar paid for nursing home assistance (and this is reported to the federal government each year, so the feds will deduct the amounts recovered, from the overall funds a given state is to receive). This is one of the strings attached by the federal government (the concept is known as the Payback Rules: the federal government expects to be repaid from whatever resources are available).

A North Dakota case gives a nice review of how the system actually works, when a person dies:

"Nathaniel Thompson received medical assistance benefits of $58,237.30 between January 1, 1991 and his death on December 20, 1992. His wife, Victoria Thompson died on September 15, 1995, leaving an estate of $46,507.98 . . . The Department (of Human Services) filed a claim against Victoria Thompson's estate for $58,237.30 in medical assistance provided to Nathaniel Thompson and $9,356.79 in interest. (In North Dakota), on the death of any recipient of medical assistance who is 55 years of age or older when the recipient received the assistance, and on the death of the spouse of such deceased recipient, the total amount of medical assistance paid on behalf of the recipient following the participants 55th birthday must be allowed as a preferred claim against the decedent's estate . . . We conclude in consideration of all the relevant statutory provisions, in light of the congressional purpose to provide medical care for the needy, reveals the legislative intention to allow states to trace the assets of recipients of medical assistance and recover the benefits paid when the recipient's surviving spouse dies." Estate of Thompson 1998 ND 226, 56NW 2nd 847 (ND1998).

Let us restate the holding of this case. During the time period when the husband was in the nursing home, DHS paid his bills, which totaled $58,237.30. He died. DHS made no claims against his estate (though that was an option available to DHS). His wife, who was never in a nursing home, died 3 years later. DHS made a creditor's claim against her estate, in the amount of $58,237.30, plus interest. The claim was allowed, and her net estate was used to pay back DHS. Her children received no inheritance.

A similar holding would probably be reached in other states. In most probate settings, government claims are treated as priority creditor's claims, and a DHS claim is a government claim. Most courts would probably follow the same logic the North Carolina court used, and permit the claim to be paid.

So exactly what can a person leave his or her heirs, after a spouse receives DHS assistance for nursing homes? Apparently, not very much, but there are a couple of techniques used, one of which is a federal program, adopted in most states, known as the Long Term Care Partnership , which exempts cash assets from being considered as a resource.

Here's how it works: you have to buy long term care insurance (from a qualified insurance company; the current list of companies varies from state to state), from a qualified insurance agent, and the policy will provide nursing home benefits (using actuarial tables, and other mathematical models, the benefits will have a current economic value; suppose that value is $150,000). Suppose the elderly person has a CD worth $150,000. Under normal circumstances, this person would be required to "spend down" the CD before he is eligible for state paid nursing home benefits. However, in this example, the man applying for benefits has a qualified long term care policy, which will pay for $150,000 in nursing home costs. This policy is not counted as a resource (it is exempt), so he qualifies for state assistance.

He goes into the nursing home, and after the insurance company pays for $150,000 in nursing home benefits, the state agency (perhaps DHS) takes over all payments. When he dies, his children will inherit $150,000, and the state DHS agency will have no right to claim that amount (even though the agency might have paid $100,000 in nursing home costs).

So what should you do? If you are insurable, and pass the other qualification criteria for state nursing home assistance, you should buy a qualified long term care policy from a qualified insurance agent.

If you are uninsurable, the question still remains: How does one plan to give an inheritance to children, if you need nursing home care? Some parents will give all of their property to their children, and hope they never have to ask the state for assistance – if assistance is required, the parents assume DHS will pay for their nursing home bills. In following such a path, and from the parents' perspective, the children will have received their inheritance (before they die), and all's well that ends well. However, the planners of our economy have considered that technique, and have determined that if such a gift were made to the children, five years before the parents ask for DHS assistance, the value of the gift is to be considered as part of the parents' assets, even though the parents don't own the property anymore (this is called the "look back" period). In addition, the Federal government and the respective state can change the rules of the game, and extend the look back period from five years to seven years or even longer. In short, the planning of today will not necessarily reflect the rules in effect tomorrow.

Other methods that might be used to reduce assets include purchasing a Medicaid-compliant life insurance policy or purchasing a Medicaid-compliant annuity. There are a handful of other methods used, to exempt the assets, but these methods -- including the VA's Aid and Attendance Program --are also beyond the scope of this book. Read the book *Checks for Vets* by Joseph Scott McCarthy for more details.

To compound matters, DHS would like to force couples to use the probate system. If the parents have decided to help their children avoid probate, by placing their property into a revocable trust, then when the parents are deceased, there is no probate estate against which to make a claim. If there is no probate estate, then DHS will not know when the person dies, and cannot make a claim against the trust assets. DHS has required (in the past) that mom and dad take their property out of the revocable trust, so that DHS can file a creditor's claim in a probate proceeding, when mom and dad are deceased.

Now that we have given you discouraging information, let us briefly mention the Affordable Health Care Act provisions on long term care. Yes, the law provides for long term care (it is known as the Community Living Assistance and Services Supports, or CLASS). This part of the statute was to provide long term health care insurance for people who need assistance at home. The problem was, how will we pay for this (as a government)? The Congressional Budget Office warned Congress that this program would only add to the deficit in 2011, the Secretary of Health and Human Services agreed, and the program was mothballed. It is still on the books, but isn't available as a solution to long term care.

From a logical perspective, the best alternative is to purchase qualified long term care insurance (in certain instances, the premiums are deductible for income tax purposes). There are some decisions to be made, however, when you consider long term care insurance. Obviously, no one wants to pay more for this type of insurance than he or she has to pay. So the insurance carriers have given us a series of questions to answer: first, do we want a lifetime benefit, a 5 year benefit, a 3 year benefit, or a 2 year benefit? The longer the coverage, the more expensive the premium. FYI, the average nursing home confinement (before death) for men is 2 years or less, for women, 3 years or less (but don't rely on these actuarial averages when you are considering insurance benefits). The second question to be answered is, when should insurance coverage begin: Medicare might pay for 20 days of your coverage, or for 100 days – but after that, the patient begins paying for his or her confinement in a nursing home. If a patient has cash resources to pay for the first 100 days (if a nursing home charges $100 a day, the total would be $10,000), then the patient should elect a 100 day deductible. If the patient only has $2,000 in cash reserves, then the patient would need a 20 day deductible. The premiums charged will be less if a longer waiting period is chosen. And finally, the patient must decide what sort of benefits are to be paid: $50 a day, $75 a day, $100 a day. The lower the amount chosen, the lower the premium.

Most policies should index the daily amount of nursing home benefits, for inflation, so if a benefit of $100 a day is selected, and inflation increases 3%, the nursing home benefit for the next year will be $103.

The last issues relate to increases in premiums and the market itself. To our knowledge, no insurance company offers a fixed premium policy anymore; each company reserves the right to increase the premiums each year, just as health insurance companies currently do. However, many of the companies are not exercising this option. If lots of claims are made, then premiums will increase each year. In addition, there is a risk an insurance company offering this type of insurance will drop out of the market. If there are too many claims made, the insurance company will simply cancel all existing policies and its insureds will have to find other carriers, assuming they are still insurable.

In conclusion, let me paraphrase Suze Orman's philosophy on this topic: long term care insurance ought to be viewed as fire insurance on a home – you hope you will never have to make a claim for a fire loss, just as you hope you will never have to make a claim for long term care. However, this issue ought to be as considered part of an estate plan. Good luck in your quest to find a good insurance carrier, if you decide that should be part of your overall estate plan.

Chapter 6: HOW TO DELAY YOUR CHILD'S INHERITANCE

Your son is 18 and your daughter is 24, and neither is financially responsible. If you die, is it wise to leave a small fortune in their hands? Since most parents think their children are financially irresponsible, the answer is "no". But how do you bring this to pass? Let's see how this works.

You can entrust their inheritance to another person, or trust company, and lay out conditions under which your son or daughter is to receive their inheritance. For instance, if you want money held back for your children's education, you can do so as part of your estate plan. When he or she reaches age 27 (or whatever age you specify), the trust will terminate and what's left will be distributed to him or her. Until then, the trustee will use (and disburse) the child's share for education related expenses.

Obviously, there are dozens of situations where an inheritance ought to be held back: your child might be receiving government benefits, and if they received an inheritance over $2,000, they might lose their government benefit. Your child might be in the midst of the divorce case, and you are fearful that an inheritance might slip into the hands of an angry in-law.

So how do you defer your child's inheritance?

The device that is commonly used to defer an inheritance is a trust. There are two types of trusts: one that is made as an independent agreement, traditionally known as a revocable inter vivos trust. There are lots of name variations for this type of trust: living trust, loving trust, revocable trust, trust agreement, and so forth. The other type trust is known as a testamentary trust, and this is a trust which is part of your last will and testament.

In both instances, there are always three parties involved: the person who creates the trust, the trustee, and the beneficiary. If an inter vivos trust is made, you will be the person creating the trust. As creator of the trust, you will be known as a Settlor, Trustor, grantor, or trust maker. In most instances, you will also be the trustee, and while you are alive, you'll be the only beneficiary (your children won't inherit until you die). When you die, the office of trustee will be assumed by whomever you named in the trust. The trustee will then hold the trust property for the benefit of the beneficiary, and the trust property will be given to the beneficiary not too long after you die.

If you prefer, you can delay the beneficiary's inheritance, and specify the conditions under which the beneficiary is to inherit: for example, you can instruct the trustee to distribute the beneficiary's share when the beneficiary reaches age 30. Until then, the trustee can make discretionary distributions for the beneficiary's support, health, maintenance and general welfare. If the beneficiary needs money, he or she can plead his or case to the trustee, and the trustee may, in its sole and absolute discretion, decide to transfer part or all of the beneficiary's share to him or her, before he or she reaches age 30. Or, the trustee may decide not to distribute all or any part of the trust property until the beneficiary attains age 30. It's all in the trustee's discretion, based on the circumstances at that time.

Trusts have been around for a long time. Inter vivos trusts were (and are) commonly used to avoid probate. To make these types of trusts work, you have to transfer property from yourself to yourself as trustee. That means your home, real estate, minerals, bank accounts, brokerage accounts, and so forth will have to be retitled in your name as trustee. If you leave certain property out of your trust, when you die, that property will go through the probate process. Thus, there are risks in creating an inter vivos trust, if the trust is not properly funded.

Testamentary trusts achieve the same objectives, but your will has to go through the probate court process. In some states, the trustee of your testamentary trust has to make an annual report to the probate court, and this increases the annual administrative expenses.

Some DIY apps and programs permit you to create testamentary trusts.

Keep in mind there are certain types of property that will not be transferred to your trust, whether it is an inter vivos trust or a testamentary trust: IRAs, annuities, other retirement plans (401k, 403B, tax sheltered annuities, etc.), and some life insurance. The beneficiary designation you make for an IRA controls who receives your IRA, and how it is to be paid out.

If you decide to create a trust, you must decide who will succeed you as trustee. You can name an individual, whether it be family member, friend or otherwise, and that person will then manage the property for the benefit of your trust beneficiary. Suffice to say, the person you name should be trustworthy (don't name a former felon, or a person with questionable character). You may name co-trustees, and they will serve in a joint capacity. You may name a corporation that has trust powers (not all corporations have the power to act as a trust company; this is a privilege granted by the banking or trust commission in your respective state).

Whoever you name as successor trustee will be paid a trustee's fee (the trustee's fee doesn't start until you die). The fee is usually 1% of the size of the trust. Thus, if the trust is worth $1 million, the trustee will be paid $10,000 per year, so long as the trust remains in effect. In addition, there will be other administrative expenses, such as accounting fees, income tax preparation fees and so forth.

In your trust, you can limit the fee for the successor trustee (e.g., my successor trustee shall receive a fee no more than 1% of the trust corpus, per year). Also consider limiting the exit fees for the trustee (some trust companies have a termination or exit fee of 5%).

Please understand there is no such thing as a perfect trustee, even at the corporate level. Your trust might contain some provision which permits the beneficiaries to remove the trustee, but this might undermine your objectives (a new trustee might decide that early termination of the trust is a good idea, contrary to your intentions; most corporate trustees will not terminate the trust until all of your specified conditions have been met).

To compound matters, if your trust is subject to the Uniform Trust Code (which has been adopted in about half of the states), the beneficiaries will have greater rights than you might think. The trust form in WillCrafter app (and the examples in this book) curtails those rights to some extent, which means, the beneficiaries ought not to be able to trump your intended distribution pattern.

If you decide to use a corporate trustee, please visit with the local trust company office to learn what fees will be charged. There are a few corporate trustees, such as Franklin Templeton Trust Company, which permit your trust estate to use your current, local financial advisor, but Franklin Templeton will serve as trust company, at a greatly reduced fee (most corporate trust companies expect a minimum fee of $5,000 a year).

The successor trustee will give the beneficiary an accounting each year, whether the trust is an inter vivos trust or a testamentary trust.

In summary, deferring a beneficiary's inheritance is probably a good thing. As you can tell from this article, selecting a successor trustee is not an easy task. Hopefully, this information will cause you to think about the weighty questions involved in creating a trust.

Chapter 7: IRAs, WILLS AND TRUSTS

Never ending questions: When will the Social Security Trust Fund run out of money? And isn't Congress going to deal with this?

We won't attempt to answer the first question, but you might be interested to learn that Congress "solved" the second problem in 1974. Here's what happened. Even though payroll taxes were increased so as to fund social security and Medicare costs, it was obvious a retiree would not be able to live on social security payments. With this in mind, Congress passed the Employee Income Retirement Security Act (ERISA), in the hope that employees would save towards their own retirement (such action would also relieve employers of funding pension plans, if they were so inclined). There were income tax lures to the employees: if the employee invested in an IRA, he or she would get an "above the line" tax deduction.

Banks, brokerage houses, and insurance companies got to work, and devised all sorts of investment packages, to induce working Americans to invest in IRAs. All of this helped the financial industry. And those who invested in an IRA had a nest egg for use in retirement years.

Since there were tax benefits given to the employee who invested in an IRA, Congress reasoned that when withdrawals were made from the IRA, the employee should pay taxes on the withdrawals. But there were limitations and restrictions placed on withdrawals: if withdrawals were made before age 59.5, the employee would have to pay a penalty (an extra 10% tax). Second, if an employee failed to make a withdrawal at age 70.5, or did not withdraw the proper amount, the employee would be taxed an additional 50% for that year (YIPES!).

There were more surprises in store for those investing in IRAs, mainly dealing with beneficiary designations. Let's start with the question, when you die, how are the IRA proceeds taxed?

First, if you name "my estate" as beneficiary of your IRA, then your personal representative (named in your will) receives the balance in your IRA account in a lump sum, but will pay 39.6% income tax (at the federal level, for amounts over $11,950) plus applicable state income taxes. Thus, your heirs could lose about half of your IRA in income taxes, if you designate "my estate" as your death beneficiary.

Second, should you name "my trust" as beneficiary of the IRA, you might reach the same result. If the trust is properly drawn, and the custodian of the IRA is a reasonable company -- not all custodians fall in this category -- then the trustee of the trust might take steps, to permit your beneficiaries to reduce the income tax impact.

Third, if you name sentient beings as IRA beneficiaries (i.e., human beings), they can elect to stretch payments over their life expectancies (yes, even new born babies can do this). Each year they will receive a sliver of your IRA, based on their age (they receive larger payments each year, as they age). In addition, humans can elect to take the money out at an accelerated pace (and pay income taxes on what's withdrawn); the option given is 5 years, but the human beneficiary can withdraw the money in one year, if he or she so desires.

What we described in the previous paragraph is known as an "inherited IRA". Spouses have one additional option, and that is, to roll over your IRA to your spouse's IRA. Since no money has been withdrawn, there are no taxes until your spouse decides to make withdrawals. Keep in mind that if you name children as your primary beneficiary, your kids are not given roll over privileges; they are required to withdraw amounts every year (even though they are under age 59.5).

Final topic: the great veto power. Unless your spouse agrees to receive less than his or her statutory share of your estate, or you have a prenuptial agreement, you cannot disinherit your spouse from your IRA. The spouse will have to sign your beneficiary designation form, if he or she is to receive less than 100% of your IRA.

Technically, your spouse is entitled to receive no more than the share he or she is guaranteed to receive, under the statute of descent and distribution (or community property rules, if applicable). The general rule of thumb is, the spouse is guaranteed a 50% share of your IRA.

The rules and regulations and articles on this topic are massive, and what we have stated is not all inclusive. But it is enough to warrant quoting the Bard of Stratford on Avon:

"Income taxes, wills, trusts and IRA Beneficiary Designations make strange bed-fellows." Shakespeare, The Tempest (paraphrased).

Chapter 8: PLANNING FOR RETIREMENT

People are living longer and are more active in their retirement years. Some of us will live to be 100. Should this become a trend, your years of retirement will be a bit longer than those of your ancestors, which means, if you retire at 65, your retirement could last 15 years or longer (if you are curious about your life expectancy, Google the topic to learn what your life expectancy is). Thus, your retirement years will be about 1/3 the life of your working career, and the years of retirement will probably have several phases, each with different needs and requirements (one of which might include long term health care insurance). As you age, you may discover your body needs more maintenance than at age 23.

Living longer may be a little frightening – especially when you try to assess how much money you will need to support the life-style you want to have during retirement. After all, you want to do more than just live long: you want to live with financial security.

Some will tell you that during retirement your annual income should be 70% to 80% of what you are currently making. Though there is an element of truth in that rule of thumb, keep in mind that everyone has different goals and needs, and the reality is, you will not be prepared to meet your needs during retirement unless you do a bit of planning.

Before you can even begin to predict how much money you'll need in retirement, you need to decide what kind of life style you want. In addition, you will have to estimate your cost of living based on today's costs, for there is no basis for knowing the cost of living 20 years from now. You should then add an inflation factor of 3 - 5% per year (multiply your annual expenses by 1.03 or 1.05), which will factor the loss of purchasing power caused by inflation, for every year from now until when you retire, and for every year thereafter.

Since this book has covered a potpourri of topics, all dealing with various aspects of your estate, we thought mentioning "retirement" plans would be of interest to you. There are many books and articles on this topic (e.g., *The Savage Number*, by Terri Savage), most of which are much better than our discussion of the topic. If you don't want to do additional reading, then here is a list of things to consider.

DEFINE YOUR OBJECTIVES

There are two basic questions which must be answered at the outset: first, where do you want to live? Some want to live in more than one place. Second, how well do you want to live? Knowing where you want to be financially and geographically during retirement is the first step towards defining your retirement goals. By evaluating your current financial position, and estimating how much money you'll need for your retirement, you can begin to build a long-term investment plan to help you reach your objectives. Thus, you should try to put a price tag on your retirement goals, which means, first estimate what you will be spending.

After you determine the expenses you will need during retirement, you must then assess your own resources: presumably, there will be some sort of social security payments available to you, and the Social Security Administration will give you an accounting of what you will be paid at various ages, when you retire (request "Your Personal Earnings and Benefit Estimate Statement" (a PEBES) from the Social Security Administration, using SSA-7004, available for download at http://www.ssa.gov/, and mail the same to P. O. Box 3600, Wilkes-Barre, PA 18767-

3600; further details on this form are available on the Internet). The maximum social security benefit for most workers who have attained maximum earnings, for the year 2013, is $3,350 per month. The amount you will actually receive depends on the amount of contributions you have made to the Social Security program. To these monthly benefits, you should also add any pensions you will receive, and any other sums to be paid to you from 401K Plans, tax sheltered annuities, IRAs, 403B Plans, and the like.

SOME THOUGHTS ON SAVING

If your retirement income is less than your projected retirement expenses, then you need to begin a savings program so as to supplement your retirement resources. There are many types of savings programs – but the two basic saving strategies used by most persons are investments in bonds and investments in stocks. Bonds, for purposes of this section of the book, include certificates of deposit, corporate bonds, savings bonds, treasury notes and bills, and treasury bonds – and for purposes of the investment triangle (discussed below), also includes life insurance, real estate, and other assets which also produce income. Before 2008 the average income produced from bonds was about 5% per year; in 2008 the Federal Reserve lowered the interest lending rate. Since those rates have been lowered, banks are not paying very much on certificates of deposit. That said, you should be able to find and purchase certificates of deposit, and "bonds" which will pay about 2% a year. Stocks are at the other end of the investment spectrum; they usually pay dividends, which are probably less than 3% per year. However, stocks usually grow in value, such that you can reasonably expect growth in a stock investment (consisting of dividends and increase in value) of about 10% per year. For planning purposes, however, and in order to be conservative, you should plan on receiving a lower growth rate.

Most persons do not directly invest in stocks – rather, they purchase mutual funds or exchange traded funds, which are securities (as are stocks and bonds) – and occasionally these are packaged under a tax sheltered annuity (insurance salesmen are normally not permitted to sell you stocks; they can sell you annuities, which are a type of investment, which owns stocks and bonds).

There are thousands of stocks available for investment, and there are also thousands of mutual funds and ETFs offered for sale (and a host of tax sheltered annuities). Since mutual funds and ETFs and annuities own a variety of investments, some of them have characteristics of a bond investment, some resemble pure stock investments, and others are designed to achieve a combination of investing in both stocks and bonds. Just as there are no guarantees on how much, if any, may be made on the purchase of an individual stock, there are also risks involved in investing in mutual funds.

THE INVESTMENT TRIANGLE

There is no perfect investment program, because we are imperfect ourselves, and by definition, we cannot create an investment model or strategy that will always work. However, the traditional investment program suggested by the investment community is this: if you prepare a statement of your net worth, including real estate, stocks, bonds, mutual funds, personal property, collectibles, registered animals, certificates of deposit, bank accounts, minerals, intellectual property such as patents and copyrights, and assign values to each category of property, your net worth ought to be apportioned as follows: 5-10% of your net worth should be in cash or cash equivalents, 40% of your net worth ought to be in stocks, and 50% of your net worth ought to be in bonds. If each category were depicted in a triangle, stock investments, which have the highest risk of loss, would be at the top of the triangle (the triangle cannot stand on its peak – it would topple over), then bonds would be the next layer of the triangle (for purposes of this triangle, bonds would include insurance, your home, real estate, CDs, and bonds) and the base of the triangle would consist of cash or cash equivalents (which have the lowest risk of loss).

The shape of your investment triangle will change as you approach your actual retirement; during retirement, you will be more interested in receiving income, than in having a stock portfolio which may not produce any income. By age 65, most couples should entertain the notion of having an investment triangle consisting of 5-10% cash and cash equivalents, 20% stocks, and 70% bonds. Using this concept, you can determine not only your net worth, you will be able to determine how much income and principal can be withdrawn from investments, over various periods of time, so as to meet your financial needs.

As you develop an investment strategy, keep in mind there is always an element of risk in any. The higher the risk, the greater reward – for you should never forget that in any investment, there is always a risk that you will not achieve a higher rate of return, due to the risky nature of any given investment. In order to formulate your own investment program, and understand more completely the risks of an investment, perhaps the most sensible solution is to find an investment advisor (or advisors, as the case may be) with whom you are comfortable, and use professional advice and counsel to formulate a program which will achieve your objectives, within your own comfort level of investments.

The following is an illustration of the investment triangle. The lower risk investments are depicted at the top of an imaginary triangle, and the higher risk investments located at the middle or base of the triangle. The chart depicts an asset allocation pattern for a person before retirement, and after retirement. Before retirement, an investment portfolio is usually riskier than after retirement.

Pre Retirement Allocation of Assets

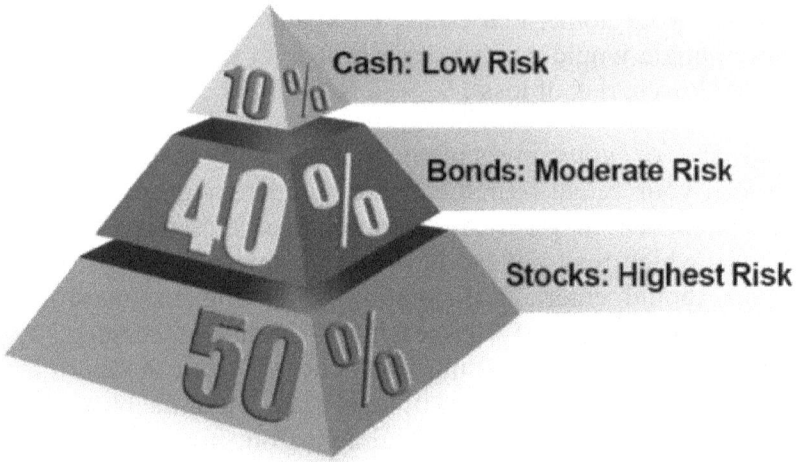

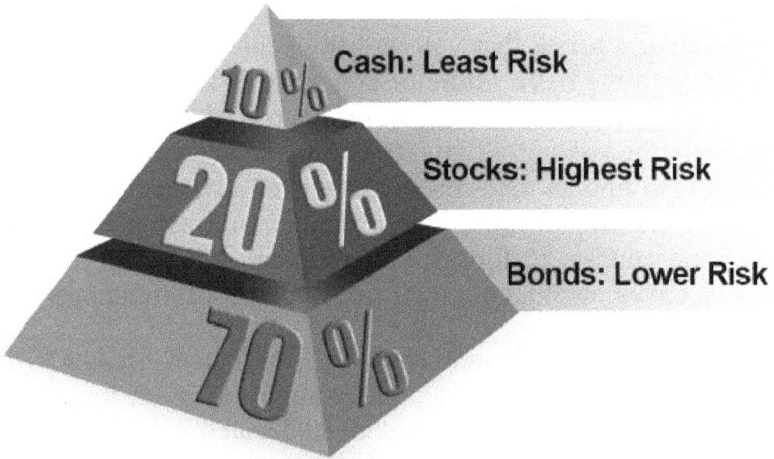

10% — Cash: Low Risk

40% — Bonds: Moderate Risk

Stocks: Highest Risk

50%

Retirement Allocation of Assets

10% — Cash: Least Risk

20% — Stocks: Highest Risk

Bonds: Lower Risk

70%

An alternative to the "investment triangle" is using a formula: subtract 100 from your age. For example, if you are 55 years old, 100 less your age is 45. Using those two numbers, you would allocate 55% of your portfolio in bonds (or investments that pay income on a fixed basis), and 45% of your portfolio in stocks or equities. Each year you will have to adjust your portfolio, to achieve an appropriate ratio. The theory in this investment formula deals with aging: as you grow older, you will be more interested in certainty, and consequently, will want to shift from the speculative nature of equities, to more conservative investments, such as bonds and certificates of deposit (or perhaps fixed annuities).

ANNUITIES

This book is not written by an insurance or investment person. With that qualification, let me try to distill the topic of annuities. During the era of Charles Dickens, an annuity was an agreement to pay another a fixed amount until that person died. Here is the example: you give me $18,000, and I sign an annuity, and promise to pay you $100 a month until you die. You are age 72. An actuary (mathematical fortune teller) tells me you will live 15 years. That means that I might have to make 180 payments to you, or $18,000. If you die at age 80, I will have paid you a total of $9,600. Under a traditional annuity, that means I have profited $8,400. You heirs receive nothing, because my promise is to you, not your heirs.

If you live to age 92, I will have paid you $22,000; thus, I will lose $4,000 on the deal.

So that's how annuities work. Now enter the 20th century and beyond, and consider how annuities are sold: the insurance industry has dominated the sale of annuities, and they sell two basic types: tax deferred annuities and fixed annuities. Let's take the easier example, fixed annuities.

A fixed annuity is a promise to pay a fixed amount of money, usually on a monthly basis, until you die. So this works just like the Victorian era annuity. The insurance companies have added several twists to the formula: they sell "joint and survivor annuities", which are promises to pay you and your spouse a fixed amount, until both of you die. When the second person dies, there is nothing left over.

A variation is a fixed annuity, life certain plus 10 years or 20 years. Translation: the insurance company will pay you a fixed amount, based on your investment (say $10,000). If you die before the annuity has been in existence for 10 years, the company will continue to pay your designated death beneficiary the same amount, until a minimum of 10 years of payments has been made.

Here's another variation: you have an IRA, and have reached age 70 ½ so you have to start withdrawing from your IRA (the "required minimum distribution"). Your IRA is with Metlife, or some other insurance company, and the insurance agents tells you to "amortize" the IRA. What this means is, you are converting the IRA into a fixed annuity, and you will be paid the same amount each month until you die.

Now let's switch gears. An insurance agent sells you a "tax deferred annuity", which is not an IRA. It is simply an investment. The insurance company might agree to pay a minimum rate of return of 2.5% a year, but you have the right to invest in a myriad of mutual funds, in the hope that your investments will grow more than 2.5%. If you are lucky or smart, the first year, your investments increase in value 7%. Since you have increased your wealth, you might ask, do I owe income taxes on this investment? The answer is no, because you have bought a tax deferred investment, meaning, until you withdraw anything from the annuity, you will not pay income taxes. You can control when you pay taxes, based on when you withdraw from the annuity.

If you buy a tax deferred annuity, keep in mind that there are penalty withdrawals, if you try to cash in your chips before 9 or

10 years. You are generally permitted to withdraw 10% of your investment a year. Also keep in mind that you cannot withdraw anything before you reach age 59 ½ (there are some exceptions to this rule).

After you reach 59.5, you might amortize the tax deferred annuity, which means, convert it to a fixed annuity, which will pay you a fixed amount each month, until you die.

There is much more to be said about annuities, but this section of the book will give you a taste of how annuities work.

LEGACIES AND INHERITANCES

A final consideration in retirement planning deals with your children: determining what amount you will leave them, and determining at what ages they will inherit your estate. It is sometimes easier to make an arbitrary decision as to what you will leave them; if your resources are insufficient to meet that objective, then you should consider purchasing life insurance to supplement that part of your retirement plan.

CONCLUSION

In conclusion, planning for retirement ought to be done as soon as possible. The best age to begin such planning is probably about 35 – but effective plans can be made at any time. We wish you success (and luck) in this very important planning process.

INDEX

www.ingramcontent.com/pod-product-compliance
Lightning Source LLC
Chambersburg PA
CBHW060627210326
41520CB00010B/1506